ASHE Higher Education Report: Volume 30, Number 5
Adrianna J. Kezar, Kelly Ward, Lisa Wolf-Wendel, Series Editors

Who Calls the Shots?

Sports and University Leadership, Culture, and Decision Making

Suzanne E. Estler with Laurie J. Nelson

Who Calls the Shots? Sports and University Leadership, Culture, and Decision Making

Suzanne E. Estler with Laurie J. Nelson

ASHE Higher Education Report: Volume 30, Number 5

Adrianna J. Kezar, Kelly Ward, Lisa Wolf-Wendel, Series Editors

ISSN 1551-6970 electronic ISSN 1554-6306 ISBN 0-7879-8076-5

The ASHE Higher Education Report is part of the Jossey-Bass Higher and Adult Education Series and is published six times a year by Wiley Subscription Services, Inc., A Wiley Company, at Jossey-Bass, 989 Market Street, San Francisco, California 94103-1741.

For subscription information, see the Back Issue/Subscription Order Form in the back of this journal.

CALL FOR PROPOSALS: Prospective authors are strongly encouraged to contact Kelly Ward (kaward@wsu.edu) or Lisa Wolf-Wendel (lwolf@ku.edu). See "About the ASHE Higher Education Report Series" in the back of this volume.

Visit the Jossey-Bass Web site at **www.josseybass.com.**

Printed in the United States of America on acid-free recycled paper.

Advisory Board

The ASHE Higher Education Report Series is sponsored by the Association for the Study of Higher Education (ASHE), which provides an editorial advisory board of ASHE members.

Contents

Executive Summary

National commissions, scholars, faculty and administrative associations, and the popular media appear to agree that something is profoundly "broke" about big-time intercollegiate athletics and their influence on colleges and universities. There are, however, conflicting opinions and perspectives on the nature of the problem(s), the potential remedies, and the degree to which they influence a broader range of colleges and universities. This volume explores how relatively independent forces constrain the ability of institutional, athletics, and faculty leaders to limit perceived excesses in the growth of intercollegiate athletics programs on their campuses and nationally. Academic and athletic cultures; historical precedent; external organizations and constituencies; external laws and regulations; and markets for athletics-related materials, entertainment, student-athletes, and professionals all bring outside forces to bear on the college culture, leadership, and decision making related to intercollegiate athletics. Finally, we examine how the unintended interactions of these forces constrain campus leadership of intercollegiate athletics and consider the resulting policy and leadership implications.

Who's in Charge? The Structure of Athletics in Higher Education

On the one hand, faculty, students, and administrators view athletics as a campus-sponsored activity. The campus builds and maintains facilities, hires and pays athletics personnel including coaches and administrators, provides budgetary support for programs, and reaps the glory or shame associated with either individual and team successes or individual and institutional misconduct.

On the other hand, intercollegiate athletics require extensive collaboration beyond campus boundaries to facilitate competition among multiple teams and institutions. Colleges and universities view agreements about the conditions and rules for competition among institutions as necessary for fairness on and off the field, especially in relation to resource allocation. The need for equitable conditions for competition has led over time to a structure of national voluntary associations and conferences of colleges and universities, each with different roots, governing the conduct of intercollegiate athletics. The effect sometimes appears to be a structure for the external control of the college athletics enterprise, with campuses operating individual franchises. The dominant governing structure is rooted in high-cost, male-oriented, high-profile sport cultures and practices dating to the early years of football in large universities. Those cultures and practices have affected less dominant men's and women's sports and smaller institutions in two ways: (1) through smaller institutions' emulation of large institutions and (2) through the application of rules designed to address needs and concerns related to big-time football and basketball to nonspectator sports and smaller institutions.

Legal and Regulatory Contexts

Externally defined laws and regulations restrict allowable actions and procedures of colleges and universities and the athletics departments within them in myriad ways. A complex web of externally imposed and internally adapted rules and routines influence campus-based athletics programs and the decision making surrounding them. They include National Collegiate Athletics Association (NCAA) regulations and those of other national associations and athletics conferences governing individual sports and rules for membership and participation. In addition, federal and state laws and regulations apply to colleges and universities and athletics programs in areas such as employment, nondiscrimination, income and sales taxes, fire regulations, and health regulations related to food concessions; further, case law governs areas such as catastrophic injury.

Laws and regulations sometimes influence campus decision making in contradictory and invisible ways through specialized and loosely coupled campus compliance channels and conflicting external demands. For example, the NCAA, which defines the rules of competition, has argued before the courts that it is exempt from federal laws that prohibit discrimination because it receives no federal funds. Yet its rules can place institutions betwixt and between NCAA regulations and nondiscrimination statutes such as the Americans with Disabilities Act and Titles VI and IX. These laws require that the mass of colleges and universities that accept federal funds not discriminate based on race, gender, or disability. Yet the NCAA, which is not a recipient of federal funds, has at times imposed regulations that may inadvertently involve violations of these laws, as sometimes illustrated by NCAA admissions standards relative to the Americans with Disabilities Act and past NCAA requirements limiting salaries of certain coaches relative to the Sherman Anti-Trust Act (1973).

Social, cultural, and political limits to the power of the legal context is demonstrated in the continuing denial of equitable opportunities for women in intercollegiate athletics a third of a century after Title IX mandated them in 1972. Women continue to be disadvantaged in college sports in participation opportunities, scholarships, facilities, budgets, pay equity for coaches, and equitable access to employment opportunities in coaching both women's and men's sports, as well as in sports administration careers.

The Social and Cultural Context

The almost invisible constraints of societal norms and values often appear to limit the power of law in relation to both gender and race. In this context, men's college sports have been a kind of bastion of socially acceptable aggressive masculinity in a world of evolving sex roles. These cultural expectations defined a particularly difficult path for the development of opportunities for women in college sports. They place even greater expectations of heterosexual sexual identity on both men and women already in a male-identified arena. The identification of sports and masculinity rendered women's sports invisible to all but a few until the courts and federal agencies began to enforce

Title IX in athletics. In relation to sexual orientation, aggressive masculinity has served as an engine both for stereotyping women athletes as lesbian for not fitting traditional sex roles and for keeping gay and lesbian athletes deeply in the closet.

College sports have also served as a cauldron for the history and complexity of U.S. racial history. Intercollegiate athletics simultaneously offer African American men an apparent opportunity for a college education and dreams of sports fame. However, they often do so by fueling false hopes of professional sports opportunities at the expense of more realistic professions. African American student-athlete graduation rates that are below those of their white counterparts' may signify exploitation or opportunities that would otherwise be inaccessible given the dynamics of race in U.S. society. The dynamics of both race and gender in college sports illustrate the degree to which the external social and cultural context shapes and influences internal practices, policies, and resource-allocation decisions.

Economic Factors in Athletics Decision Making

Economic forces related to athletics decision making and culture have moved historically toward increasing commercialization, including but not limited to gate receipts, athletic equipment sales, facilities construction, trademark licensing, concessions, coaching and professional labor markets, advertising, and media contracts. Athletics are also identified indirectly with markets for student enrollments, philanthropy, legislative financial support, and media visibility. Perceptions of market forces related to athletics may be as important as the reality in influencing athletics decision making, as the poorly substantiated assumption of fundraising and enrollment benefits related to a successful sports program illustrates.

Although athletics is an enterprise on the margins of the teaching and knowledge production role of the university, its web of external connections and responsibilities produces internal dilemmas, ambiguities, and puzzles related to core institutional decisions. In the aggregate, the numerous apparently minor decisions made over time through diverse links to the external environment leave leaders with a predefined set of limits when faced with major decisions. These limits to decision options are not necessarily coordinated, consistent, nor strategically wise. Because of the complexity and invisibility of these forces, institutions and their leaders make decisions that appear to make little sense to some observers and participants. These processes confound traditional rational views that implicitly shape expectations of decision making and leadership—expectations echoed throughout the literature calling for athletics reform. An understanding of the nature and role of external forces influencing intercollegiate athletics allows new strategies for planning and prioritizing sports within the college or university. Thus institutional leaders might be more able to address the disproportionate increases in athletics spending (the athletics arms race) while making greater sense of decision processes creating it.

Strategies

The complex interplay of forces influencing intercollegiate athletics and the perceptions of those viewing it affirm existing leadership strategies and suggest some newer ones. The literature already addresses concepts such as coalition building, presidential control of athletics governance, and a variety of rules reforms. This analysis adds consideration to the less visible and less intentional social and cultural contexts profoundly affecting structure, laws and regulations, and the economics of college sports. Leadership strategies include focusing on culture and symbols; opportunistically using events to strengthen intra-institutional ties between athletics, the academic core, and student affairs supports on the campus; aggressively pursuing coalitions externally; and assuring vigilance (and reform when necessary) within the institution, conferences, and national associations.

Foreword

Early in my academic career, my father-in-law used to belabor me with his perception of the demise of the University of Chicago as a significant academic institution. His evidence: the university had withdrawn from big-time intercollegiate athletics. From the lofty perch of my academic pretensions, I smiled at his innocence. In this book, Suzanne Estler reminds us that I should have smiled at my own.

Professor Estler is an experienced university administrator, a student of higher education, and a thoughtful organizational analyst. Most of all, she is a careful and subtle scholar who paints a richly textured and theoretically informed portrait of intercollegiate athletics in U.S. universities without overburdening the reader with technical terms or statistical pyrotechnics. It is not easy to write a book that speaks both to the intelligent practitioner and to the intelligent scholar, but Sue Estler has done so.

As she makes clear, U.S. universities are complex institutions, and appreciating the role of intercollegiate athletics in them requires a nuanced understanding of cultures, rules, histories, incentives, and people. Much of this complexity is lost in conventional contemporary accounts, which are often written from the point of view of one of the contending groups in the debate over college athletics—faculty members, athletics department representatives, advocates for gender or racial equity in universities or in athletics, college presidents, former college presidents, and so on. They seem more committed to the proclamation of simple theses or the promulgation of simple nostrums than to comprehension of the phenomena.

Professor Estler's book is different. She is a veteran of the intercollegiate athletics wars and carries some scars to prove it. She writes as a participant, but the book is at the same time also written with the understanding of a student of organizations. Four central ideas in particular seem to me to place analysis in Professor Estler's book on a level of scholarly seriousness above that of many related treatises.

First, she sees the university as a profoundly *political* institution. Universities are coalitions of diverse interests, held together less by a shared purpose from which everything else is derived than by negotiations and trades among conflicting groups.

Second, she sees the composition of a university coalition as being continually renegotiated by the *entrepreneurial* spirit of institutions and their leaders, seeking advantage in competition with other universities and with other social institutions. University groups are continually scanning the environment for possible allies.

Third, she sees the implementation of coalition agreements as producing organizational *rules* and stimulating the elaboration of offices and networks of professionals to interpret the rules. The university is a system of rules, and rules proliferate professionalism and bureaucracy.

Fourth, she sees the university generally and its activities in athletics specifically as highly *symbolic.* This extends to the interpretations given to almost every element of university athletics and administrative action, but it is particularly evident in the relations between the symbols of gender and the symbols of sports.

The development of these and other ideas reflects the fact that the author has taken time. U.S. universities and their procedures are implicated in one of the travesties of scholarship—the production of pseudo-scholarship, rushed to completion without serious thought and published without prospect of significance. Thoughtful scholarship devours time, and we should be grateful when a scholar, despite the incentives to rush things, takes the time necessary to understand the questions thoroughly and to digest the research effectively. Professor Estler has been patient; she has been thorough; and she has written a serious book.

In short, the book is filled with information, analysis, and wisdom that comes from immersing a smart and perceptive person in a complicated world. It should be read not only by scholars but also by university administrators. For the latter, of course, knowledge is a mixed blessing. At least since Shakespeare persuaded Hamlet to comment on the way "the native hue of resolution is sicklied o'er with the pale cast of thought," leaders have struggled with the dilemma of reconciling desires for simple, decisive action with knowledge about the complexities of situations and institutions. Far from resolving that dilemma, Professor Estler's book probably accentuates it, as knowledge usually does. Rather than offer simple solutions based on glib clichés, it invites informed judgment based on carefully considered scholarship and experience.

James G. March
Professor Emeritus
Stanford University

Preface and Acknowledgments

Almost since their inception, college sports have coexisted in uneasy alliances with the academic missions of the institutions housing them. Occasionally, fissures in the alliances either derail or boost the careers of presidents, coaches, and athletics directors and tarnish or burnish the reputations of their institutions. In the dramas of higher education and competitive sports, the experiences and values of the actors' respective institutions shape their realities and worldviews. Reflecting those experiences, people of goodwill can draw very different conclusions from the same information—and more likely, they are exposed to different information about the same issues. These differences in perspective and information, leavened by the confluence of opportunities, challenges, participants, and occasions for decision at given times, leaves chance a major actor in the evolution of the complex relationship between sports and academe. Strategies for change, then, must account for unplanned and unintended circumstances, chance, and differences in perception of the same events in order to be effective.

Consistent with this observation, this work reflects my personal and academic belief in the importance of unplanned behavior and unintended consequences in the outcome of organized human endeavors. These beliefs were born of experience and influenced theoretically by James G. March and an evolving crew of "cellar-rats" in the basement of Stanford's Cubberly Hall. Jim's lessons in the tolerance of ambiguity, the joys of finding a different kind of order in apparent disorder, and leadership embodied in doing the right thing regardless of expectations for success have served both my scholarship and life. For the degree to which his influence is reflected here, I am deeply grateful.

To the extent I may have wreaked havoc on those concepts in viewing college sports, I'll trust in his forgiveness if not amusement. More immediately, I am particularly appreciative of Jim's willingness to bring a perceptive eye and useful feedback to the reading of this manuscript.

Jim also taught that collaboration and interaction leaven good scholarship. In that tradition, a number of colleagues and students contributed to this effort over several years. Each has made it better, though none but the authors bear responsibility for the outcome. This examination of the relationship between intercollegiate athletics and university culture and decision making was partially inspired by a decade as director of equal opportunity at a predominantly white land-grant institution with a National Collegiate Athletics Association (NCAA) Division I-AA athletics program. This experience on the president's staff demonstrated the time, attention, institutional energy, and institutional capital (human, political, and financial) required to sustain the intercollegiate athletics enterprise and its connections throughout the university. Those demands and dynamics raised intriguing and persistent questions that resulted in this effort. Shared experience with a number of University of Maine presidents, vice presidents, athletics directors, and coaches offered practical views into the intersection between athletics and academics that they may well be unaware they provided. They nevertheless gave a reality base from which to assess concepts from the literature related to athletics, gender, race, leadership, and the peculiar challenges of Division I-AA sports. For those insights, I am grateful to Walt Abbott, Janet Anderson, Judi Bailey, Greg Brown, Jack Cosgrove, John Diamond, Stu Haskell, John Hitt, Fred Hutchinson, Terry Kix, Dale Lick, Joanne Palombo McCallie, Mike Ploszek, Charles F. Rauch, Trish Roberts, Julia Watkins, Bob Whelan, Kevin White, and Margaret Zillioux. I'm appreciative to Jim Fairweather for the inspiration to pursue this effort as a mechanism to bridge the insights from experience and the bodies of scholarship that might inform it. The manuscript was improved by the wisdom of Jennifer Lee Hoffman, John Thelin, and Doug Toma, who offered particularly helpful comments from beyond Maine, as did several anonymous reviewers.

Graduate students in student development in higher education at the University of Maine either opened their minds to the role of athletics in the university or blessed us in sharing reflections on their own experiences as scholarship football players and athletics staff. I appreciate the following students' contributions in helping sift and consider a vast literature or to take the time to read and respond: Elizabeth Barry, Jennifer Boynton-Allen, Aaron Dashiell, Chris Dayss, Gennaro DeAngelis, Melissa Komasz, Catherine Reader, E. J. Roach, Deb Rountree, Lauri Sidelko, and Ako Stafford. A University of Maine feminist writing group provided deadlines, time, rigorous feedback, and enthusiasm; thanks go to Elizabeth Allan, Pamela Dean, Amy Fried, Andrea Hawkes, Mazie Hough, Kristin Langellier, Pauleena MacDougall, and Marli Weiner. Sandra Haggard, Judi Monroe, and Sue Simpson served as gifted summer surrogates for the writing group on Swans Island. Marli, Mazie, Sandra, and Elizabeth went above and beyond in deferring their own work to read the almost full manuscript on short notice—one last time. Colleagues in the University of Maine College of Education and Human Development brought both experience and academic insight to the review of drafts and the discussion of ideas: Elizabeth Allan, David Brown, Gordon Donaldson, Diane Hoff, Anne Pooler, Sue Tyler, and Nancy Yoder. At the University of Maine, I am grateful too for a Faculty Research Fund summer research grant supporting this work.

Finally, heaven will hold a special place for the following people:

- Laurie Nelson, whose knowledge, research experience, and focus allowed her to join this project after its inception and give it insight, organization, and enthusiasm. Although I conceptualized the project, did the research, and wrote the primary drafts, Laurie's conceptual and organizational contributions came to be far more substantial than simple editing, and thus she is recognized in the authorship designation.
- Elizabeth Allan, for her initial inspiration and her unfailing support as the project unfolded. She has become an ideal colleague and a good friend.
- Kimberly Smith, whose timely interest and attention to detail helped tie it all up.
- Adrianna Kezar, whose vision, encouragement, patience, and editorial hand assured an idea would come to fruition.
- Paula Johnson, who was there every step of the way with support, sustenance, patience, and multiple reminders that there is life after scholarship.

Introduction and Overview

"IN THE [1993] CHAMPIONSHIP GAME, three Lake Superior State goals in the second period staked the Lakers to a 4-2 lead entering the third period. But Montgomery and Kariya would answer, forever etching their mark in championship history, as Montgomery scored three goals in a span of 4:35, all three goals set up by Kariya, to give UMaine its first national title and a come from behind 5-4 victory" (University of Maine, 2004, p. 80).

The miraculous journey to a 1993 national hockey championship raised statewide visibility and expectations for the National Collegiate Athletics Association (NCAA) Division I-AA athletics programs of our small land-grant university. Many observers attributed enrollment growth the following year to the visibility and pride that the hockey championship generated throughout the state. Pride faded, however, when an unrelenting series of seemingly unrelated alleged violations of NCAA rules surfaced in the subsequent year. Each revelation, no matter how minor, triggered a media firestorm weak in facts but high in speculation. Faculty and administrators who had paid relatively little attention to athletics over the years now faced a public crisis in confidence affecting the institution as a whole. We were not a big-time institution. Yet the media image, however inaccurate, of an institution out of control tarred our reputation beyond both athletics and the immediate geographic surroundings. The fears of faculty and administrators were realized when enrollments dropped the next year as the NCAA investigation stretched on.

What went wrong? How did a small institution generally well regarded for its integrity go from a national championship to NCAA probation? Any attempt to explore that question quickly leads to others about the place of intercollegiate athletics within U.S. higher education and to innumerable sagas of far greater triumphs and tragedies in big-time institutions. This monograph reviews the literature of intercollegiate athletics through lenses informed by organizational theory to understand better why colleges and universities continue to grow athletics programs to new financially, physically, and ethically challenged levels despite their own stated priorities to the contrary. It argues that structural, legal, economic, social, and cultural forces external to the institution create a kind of invisible hand governing the institution of college sports almost independently of the colleges and universities they represent. This exploration leads to an understanding of the unique role of football as a social institution embodying masculine culture ultimately shaping the foundational structure and regulation of college sports regardless of college or university size or the specific sport in question.

The 1994 campus experience related to NCAA violations forced leaders to turn their attention to athletics-related themes common to colleges and universities across the country and illustrated the complexity of the demands that such athletics-related scenarios placed on campus leaders. Further, popular and academic media affirmed the degree to which we shared the struggles to manage the athletics enterprise with peer institutions. Like many of those institutions, we occupied a niche in higher education in which the financial ante for engaging in Division I athletics was high in scholarships, travel, and facilities. At the same time, our revenues consistently fell far below costs, with low seating capacities in our facilities compounded by a campus and community culture more interested in hockey and basketball than football.

Our relatively modest program nevertheless hosted a range of local, regional, and national interests with substantial financial stakes in the athletics status quo. Travel agencies, sports equipment retailers, bus companies and airlines, motels, refreshment concessions; coaching, training, and support staffs; and of course, generations of mostly male student-athletes whose skills allowed them access to a college education shared economic stakes in the size and nature of the athletics program. Simultaneously, faculty on campus expressed deep concern about priorities reflected in the university's increasing athletics expenditures while reducing or eliminating academic programs in the face of systemwide budget cuts. The unfolding athletics drama involved

NCAA rules violations and an associated media firestorm, financial constraints across the campus fueling animosity toward athletics, and growing community investment in the sports programs. The drama demanded intense attention from the central administration.

Prior history had not prepared the campus well for dialogue related to athletics. The academic culture over previous years demanded that we not talk too much about athletics because such talk would appear to draw even more attention to a nonacademic aspect of the university that far more easily gained public attention than did more central research, teaching, and service. Thus the sports program was like the metaphorical elephant in the living room, signifying a family crisis that affects all the family members but that none dare discuss. But when the media firestorm broke out, members of every constituency on and off campus had something to say about our sports program.

The Problem in Decision Making Related to Athletics

Though details may differ, the central dilemma of the vignette beginning this chapter is familiar to campus leadership: how to reap educational, social, and economic benefits from a strong athletics program without cost to the institution's academic and moral integrity. Facing financial constraints, campus leaders have often looked to athletics as a source of enhanced name recognition, or branding, to increase enrollments, donors, and associated revenues. They had historic precedent in the fortunes of institutions such as Yale, Harvard, the University of Chicago, and Notre Dame, which had built enrollment and ultimately academic strength on the visibility that early twentieth-century football generated.

Contemporary university presidents have often tried to follow in these footsteps without reckoning with the potential wrath of those faculty, students, legislators, and members of governing boards who may view increased commitment to sports as both frivolous spending and a betrayal of central academic values. The president who challenges the size of a sports program may incur the anger of boards, community members, and alumni whose loyalty to the institution is based on their connections to athletics teams.

A campus leader, especially at a Division I institution, must straddle the line between two sets of values related to athletics that can foster very different decisions. At the extremes, one set of values extols "the pursuit of athletic competition as an essential component of superior higher-education institutions" (Lombardi and others, 2003, p. 3). Another views "this American passion for organized college sports competition as an egregious attachment to the body academic whose removal should be the goal of every serious person" (p. 3). For example, faced with NCAA violations by a popular coach, a leader might dismiss him in order to signal a strong commitment to the institution's teaching and research core. Alternatively, the leader might decide to impose no penalty or a lesser one in deference to the coach's prior history and to the support that alumni, past and potential donors, community members linked to the university through their identification with sports, legislators, and the institutional governing board all express. In either case, there may well be a subsequent outcry expressing the values previously unheard. The maelstrom, involving the institution as a whole, would likely have far more media coverage than a major academic achievement.

The visibility illustrates that despite a role ostensibly on the margins of the institution's academic mission, athletics demand the primary attention of those charged with decision making at the institution's center. The manner in which a president, athletics director, board, or faculty leadership pursues either horn of the dilemma can ultimately either sabotage leadership credibility or show her or him to be a hero of institutional integrity.

This clashing of values engenders a decision-making process that poses a particular leadership challenge related to athletics programs in higher education. The impact of external dynamics on internal institutional decision making compounds the challenge of managing the dilemmas implicit in a nonacademic program with extensive power and influence. In many cases, decisions that affect the relationship between the athletics program and its external structural, legal, and cultural environment do not occur daily through central administrative deliberations. Instead, like other university units bridging the university and the environment, athletics decisions are often low profile, decentralized, and incremental. Yet those decisions can have long-term consequences involving the institution as a whole.

Interpretations of the Problems

The decision-making challenge begins with divergent interpretations of the problems surrounding athletics programs. Many faculty, students, trustees, and legislators view growing athletics programs as a challenge to academic programs and institutional integrity. At the same time, others identify with their university or undergraduate institution based on the visibility of football or basketball teams. In some cases, a college or university is publicly identified with less overtly commercial sports such as crew, track and field, or swimming. And the smallest of local-business institutions may even depend on the income produced by team and fan travel, motels and hotels, concessions, and athletics equipment. Print and broadcast media attend more readily to a college or university's trials on the gridiron than to the faculty's more esoteric research breakthroughs. A review of the literature of intercollegiate athletics suggests apparent universal agreement that something is profoundly "broke" about the enterprise (although satisfied participants rarely write books and articles). However, beneath this apparent consensus lies an array of disparate opinions and perspectives on the nature of the problem(s) and the potential solutions to fix them. Duderstadt (2000), for example, lists athletics stakeholders including coaches, athletics directors, and associated staffs; the print and broadcast news and entertainment industries; sports apparel manufacturers and retailers; boosters and fans; student-athletes themselves; and the governance structure of the university including faculty, governing boards, and presidents. Scholars, students, and critics of the enterprise might round out Duderstadt's list.

Scholars and stakeholders have produced a large body of literature documenting the century-long efforts to reform the athletics enterprise, the current challenges to reform, and why reform matters (Thelin, 1994; Shulman and Bowen, 2001; Sack and Staurowsky, 1998). Although presidents are able to reflect with insider perspectives, scholars and study commissions may be less burdened with histories to analyze or defend. The literature advocating athletics reform further illustrates the diversity of stakeholders in those who produce the reports and those whom the reports cite as keys to successful reform efforts.

Presidential Perspectives

Caught in the dilemmas presented by athletics decision-making, seasoned presidents have been exposed firsthand to the complexities and dynamics that college sports present. Retired presidents with perspectives often forged in the fires of athletics controversy have produced a literature on college sports. Works by Campbell (2000), DiBiaggio (1991), Lapchick and Slaughter (1994), Gray (1996), Hesburgh and Alvino (1995), and Shulman and Bowen (2001), for example, represented the presidencies of the University of Oklahoma, University of Michigan, Michigan State, University of Chicago, Notre Dame, Washington State, University of Maryland, and Princeton University, respectively. All are institutions that have been identified historically—if they are not at the present—as major names in college sports. In several cases, their presidents left after conflicts with boards over either integrity in collegiate athletics or inordinate attention to college sports.

The literature by recent presidents captures many of the complexities of campus politics and university athletics, if sometimes as a defense of their own records. Duderstadt (2000) blames the media for creating the appearance of all college sports as represented by big-time football and basketball programs, with both well-paid celebrity coaches and soon-to-be-professional athletes. In reality, he notes, there is great diversity among colleges and universities and very different histories associated with various sports even on a single campus.

These campus leaders identify three consistent themes. First is the steep financial escalation associated with intercollegiate athletics as each athletics department seeks the elusive level playing field and perhaps a competitive edge. The escalation is fueled with the effort to keep up with peer institutions, requiring bigger and better-equipped facilities, more and higher-paid coaches, elaborate and well-staffed training rooms, and extensive university-wide compliance systems, a dynamic discussed further in the chapter "Economics and the Athletics System." The second theme is the threat to academic integrity associated with the commercialization and competitiveness of college sports. The third theme is the risk of exploiting student-athletes for their physical skills without regard to their academic needs (discussed further in the chapter "The Social and Cultural Context").

Some of these presidents further note that these increased costs are compounded by the large investment in athletics scholarships and the automatic increase in their cost each time the university raises the tuition. For example, an athletics department budget with five hundred scholarship athletes would need to increase by $500,000 if tuition increased by $1,000 in a given year.

Those with presidential experience also typically speak to the potential conflict between academic values and athletics values. Like many critics, for example, they express concern regarding the degree to which compromised admissions standards and lower academic expectations for student-athletes, or even the appearance of lower standards, compromise academic integrity. Yet the former presidents also show enhanced awareness of the range of stakeholders in the athletics enterprise, many of whom depend on sports for their livelihoods.

Board Perspectives

The Association of Governing Boards (AGB) released a major report entitled *Statement on Board Responsibilities for Intercollegiate Athletics* in 2004. The report addressed eight major foci relevant to board responsibility regarding athletics: "General oversight responsibilities, presidential authority, athletics department mission, fiscal responsibility, academics and student-athlete welfare, compliance, personnel, and communications" (p. 4).

Gerdy (2001, p. 1) appeals to trustees to join presidents in leading the charge to reform, noting that "To characterize the marriage of athletics and American higher education as having long been 'strained' is an understatement." He further observes that attempts to reform athletics "are almost as much a part of higher education's history as the classroom lecture."

Foundation and Commission Perspectives

Many reports, articles, and books have outlined concerns regarding college sports and offered proposals for reforms to align them more clearly with the academic mission of colleges and universities. Thelin (1994) documents the early history of these efforts. More recently, reports from the Knight Foundation Commission on Intercollegiate Athletics (Knight Commission) (1991, 2001) and the Mellon Foundation studies by Shulman and Bowen (2001) and Bowen and Levin (2003) are among the most comprehensive. In addition, each project spawned additional position papers with in-depth analysis of various aspects of the issues under study. These foundations, in turn, have produced new organizations to advocate for change in intercollegiate sports. The Mellon Foundation has sponsored the founding of the College Sports Project, originated through a gathering of the presidents of 130 liberal arts colleges, seeking to ensure "that coaches and athletes are integrated into campus life and that athletes ought to be academically representative of other students" (Suggs, 2004a). The formation of the College Sports Project signals the clear concerns among Division III institutions about the escalating influence and costs of athletics.

Faculty Perspectives

Individual faculty members write about college sports as both scholars of sport and advocates for reform (Thelin, 1994; Chu, 1989; Sack and Staurowsky, 1998; and Sperber, 1990). Faculty have also worked collectively, for example, forming the Drake Group in 2000 ("defend academic integrity in the face of commercialized college sport" (n.p., 2004). More recently, the Coalition for Intercollegiate Athletics (COIA) was founded in 2002 as a coalition of faculty senates from NCAA Division I institutions seeking "to become a faculty voice in the national debate over the future of college sports" (COIA, 2004). COIA works with the AGB and the NCAA. All three groups are committed to building coalitions in order to meet their objectives more effectively.

The deep dilemmas the athletics enterprise has posed to higher education over the years have fostered many other reform attempts that subsequent chapters will discuss. The national committees and commissions dating from the origins of the NCAA in 1906 to the latest Knight Commission report (2001) have advocated for the reform of intercollegiate athletics to assure amateurism and reduce spending, commercialization, and unethical practices. Central to most of those reports' recommendations are calls for presidential leadership, with the implicit assumption that university presidents hold an element of control over the enterprise (Thelin and Wiseman, 1989). Typical recommendations common to several of these efforts include the following:

Fostering strong presidential, board, and faculty leadership

Building coalitions across institutions with coordinated efforts to reduce athletics spending

Integrating student-athletes more fully into the academic life of the college or university

Cutting back on playing and practice schedules

Reducing or eliminating athletics scholarships

Encouraging the establishment of minor league systems in the National Basketball Association and the National Football Association

Instituting presidential control of national athletics governance organizations

Incorporating standards for athletics into regional higher education accreditation reviews of colleges and universities

Expanding presidential oversight of athletics programs and budgets

Expanding board committee oversight of athletics programs

Today's NCAA regulations reflect the consequences of a century of reform designed to assure fair competition and the ethical treatment of student-athletes. These regulations have grown at an exponential rate, with each transgression not apparently covered by existing rules producing a new rule. As a result, the *NCAA Manual* (2004), to which coaches, administrators, student-athletes, and even potential applicants are accountable, numbers close to five hundred pages. The manual represents a potential minefield of possible unintentional violations. The complex and convoluted structure to achieve order and fairness in college sports has become one instrument through which the external demands of the athletics enterprise appears to shape campus policies and practices. Subsequent chapters will elaborate on the ways in which the complex dynamics of structural, legal, sociocultural, and economic contexts have stymied reform efforts over the years.

Theoretical Context

Addressing the campus leadership conundrum related to athletics requires organizational lenses that go beyond "great man" theories, hierarchical theories, and theories assuming the dominance of faculty governance of colleges and universities. Even in recognizing the complexities of politics and external engagement in college sports, major reports and reviews ultimately conclude by calling for presidents, faculty, or trustees (depending on whom the authors view as the ultimate authority) to clean up college athletics without regard for the dominance of external forces.

Colleges and universities can be viewed as institutions steeped in sometimes competing values, goals, means for achieving goals, and embedded traditions (Cohen and March, 1974; Baldridge, Curtis, Ecker, and Riley, 1977; Birnbaum, 1991). In order to accommodate these competing goals, values, and structures, institutions have grown to resemble more a collection of semiautonomous organizations than a single hierarchical monolith.

This view contrasts with cultural norms of leadership, rationality, and organizational hierarchy supporting expectations for campus leaders to halt the athletics arms race and assure a place for athletics appropriate to the college or university's educational mission. Based on traditional views of leadership and organization, campus participants often assume that outcomes are the result of intended actions by those with campus-level authority.

The contrast between expectations for authoritative leadership and the reality of outcomes shaped by a myriad of forces beyond the control of any one person or group reflects implicit assumptions consistent with neo-institutional theory. In this case, we would view athletics as a societal institution shaped by dynamics beyond university boundaries that may affect internal decision-making and culture in ways not obvious on the surface. External structures, laws and regulations, social and cultural values, and economic forces differentially affect athletics departments and college and university culture. Participants construct different meanings of what they see. Neo-institutional theory with roots in sociology, political science, economics, and cognitive psychology offers a perspective assuming different realities as actors interpret their experience in different ways (Scott, 2001; Powell and DiMaggio, 1991).

Many of these theorists look at organizations as both shaped by and acting on the larger environment of organizations and social institutions in which they function. Shared elements within this school of thought include (1) an interest in the nonrational impact of the social and cultural context on organizational processes; (2) the assumption that realities are socially constructed, that is, the realities perceived by participants vary depending on the participants' experience, values, and position; (3) a respect for the role of history in shaping the present context; and (4) a belief that the complex interplay of values, history, and external and internal organizational dynamics requires a rich contextual understanding of unique cases to infer broader theoretical meanings.

This perspective captures the degree to which participants and stakeholders have differing windows into the athletics enterprise and the institution. They literally see athletics and its place in the college or university in different ways. We can imagine some of the differences in perception: the football coach in a Division I-A program sees a different picture of athletics than does a faculty member in the English department or a soccer player in the same institution. The parent of an inner-city high school basketball player will see sports and life opportunities differently than will a prep school, all-state basketball point guard with privileged access to a world of professional opportunity beyond sports. Women's sports participants, coaches, students, and fans may well view the athletics enterprise as one in which it is still difficult to be seen and supported.

A view of the college or university as shaped by and shaping the external environment through their interactions might look like a busy office building housing a variety of enterprises with varying missions, a variety of leaders and leadership styles, and different views and points of access to the outside world. The issues that each considers important vary from unit to unit; what they see depends on the window from which they are looking. In other words, how one constructs the reality of the building and the external environment depends on where one sits.

Athletics often lie at the center of campus dynamics related to academic standards, race, gender, reputation, finance, community relations, politics, priorities, legal responsibilities and liabilities, and ethical responsibilities. Yet athletics are rarely reflected in the literature of higher education related to these areas. This review addresses leadership, policy, and research implications for institutions, the NCAA and other national associations, and various stakeholder groups stemming from a clearer understanding of the intersection between intercollegiate athletics, campus leadership and governance, and the external environment. Most importantly, it provides a relatively brief tool enabling stakeholders and participants in any given niche in the intercollegiate sports enterprise to see their vantage point as part of a complex whole.

Structure of the Monograph

Attending to this perspective, this monograph seeks, through a synthesis of existing literature, to understand better how external forces operating through an enterprise on the academic margins can lead institutions and their leaders to make decisions that appear to many observers to make little sense relative to the institution's mission. Through the athletics enterprise, we consider the ways in which interacting forces produce ambiguities and puzzles confounding traditional rational views of decision making. This review focuses on intercollegiate athletics. The resulting analysis, however, has implications for the leadership and governance challenge to assure the integration of any unit with deep interactions with the external environment.

An array of external forces influencing decision-making and leadership related to intercollegiate athletics frames the subsequent structure of this monograph. The next chapter describes the formal national and regional structures of intercollegiate sport that provide a framework within which individual campuses collaborate in engaging in the sports enterprise. The subsequent chapters address the legal and regulatory, social and cultural, and economic contexts of college athletics, respectively. The final chapter explores the intended and unintended effects of the interaction of those forces on campus leadership and decision making. The strategic implications of the analysis of intercollegiate athletics and university decision making, leadership, and culture frame the conclusion.

Significance to Higher Education Study and Practice

This exploration of the literature of intercollegiate athletics and university leadership and culture provides new ways of understanding the causes and leadership implications for the disproportionate influence of college sports on U.S. campuses. It also provides new lenses for understanding the apparent inability of campus leaders to lend to athletics a consistent pattern of institutional integration and control. An understanding of the nature and role of external forces on institutional decision making allows new strategies for planning and prioritizing intercollegiate athletics.

Finally, the case of college and university athletics has theoretical implications for considering the ways in which a full range of units interact semiautonomously with the institution's external environment. Sponsored research units, as well as auxiliary services such as food services and bookstores, centers for performing arts, and museums, are examples of units that share some organizational dynamics with athletics. Each represents a direct window to the external environment through commerce, community relations, professional associations and values, and an externally derived flow of resources. Although focusing on athletics, the theoretical analysis resulting from this review has implications for viewing colleges and universities as a whole as they interact through subunits with their external environments.

This monograph serves as a primer for intercollegiate athletics and the institutions that house them; it is meant to empower stakeholders in college sports. Campus-based constituents, whether designated campus leaders, administrators, faculty, or students, will find a framework and information to help them understand the complexity of intercollegiate athletics, associated issues, and their place in both higher education and U.S. culture and economy.

The following chapters describe first the structures for the governance of college sports. They then describe the influence on both colleges and universities and national governing structures of the external web of laws and regulations, the social and cultural context surrounding both athletics and higher education, and the economic dynamics among the many markets associated with college sports.

The Athletics System in Higher Education

SOME YEARS AGO, I attended a National Collegiate Athletic Association (NCAA) workshop on Title IX. It was readily apparent that the workshop was well planned, well executed, and useful to those of us often at the front lines of campus concerns regarding gender equity in athletics. I quickly realized, however, that this was not a campus-based setting when the warm welcome from the NCAA official referred to the welfare of "*our* student-athletes," words prompting campus-based faculty and administrators to think, *No, they're* our *students, not yours!*

Of course, we were all correct. Boards, administrators, and faculty at individual campuses sponsoring sports teams naturally see the college or university as responsible for teams and the students who compete on them. At national athletic associations, or in the dozens of conferences coordinating intercollegiate competition, professional staff who have committed their careers to facilitating intercollegiate athletics see the student-athlete as their *raison d'être.* Although both groups may see students as central to their work, very different experiences, interests, and professional goals and values may shape the meaning of that perception. The different professional associations with which postsecondary faculty, administrators, and athletics staff affiliate often help define and reinforce those perceptions of athletics, the student-athlete, and the place of athletics in the institution. As the primary historic arena in which colleges and universities voluntarily collaborate, athletics have demanded regional and national governance structures to assure fair and balanced competitions. These structures have been central to the development of a corps of athletics professionals and related professional associations affecting and affected by campus-level culture and decision processes related to intercollegiate athletics.

Colleges and universities formed collaborative associations in the nineteenth century to define terms of institutional competition, game rules, and eligibility for competition (Hardy and Berryman, 1982). This chapter explores the contemporary college athletics system and its roots, describing the major associations governing college sports and the contexts producing them, including the NCAA, the now extinct Association for Intercollegiate Athletics for Women (AIAW), the National Association for Intercollegiate Athletics (NAIA), and the National Junior College Athletic Association (NJCAA). The chapter assumes linkages between these organizations' origins and their current missions that are essential to understanding contemporary relationships between campus decision making and culture on the one hand and intercollegiate athletics on the other. The chapter further addresses the role of regional conferences and the Bowl Championship Series in shaping the contemporary structure of intercollegiate athletics. In considering the historical context that produced today's system, it addresses the power of football in defining the current structure of college sports, the loss of self-governance in women's sports, and the diffusion of practices associated with spectator sports at large universities to sports programs throughout all levels of higher education.

Contemporary Governing Organizations

The NCAA, the NAIA, and the NJCAA govern most intercollegiate athletics. With a few smaller, more specialized groups, they are voluntary, unincorporated associations of member colleges and universities that hire professional and support staff to conduct their business. Table 1 describes each association, its origins, purpose, approximate membership, and, in the case of the NCAA, the number of student-athletes by division. The missions of national associations have grown over time to defining and monitoring game and eligibility rules, sponsoring championships, and serving as hubs for an increasing number of coaching and athletics administrative professional organizations (Hardy and Berryman, 1982).

As illustrated in Table 1, the NCAA is the largest of the three associations, with 1,028 member colleges and universities in 2004 organized in three divisions reflecting differences in program size, mission, budget, and facilities. Division I-A is most identified with big-time intercollegiate athletics, with membership requiring threshold levels for numbers of sports, scholarships, and size of facilities. Division III is at the other end of the NCAA membership continuum and emphasizes the value of participation and precludes athletic financial student financial aid. Among the various associations, the NCAA has the largest budgets and institutional enrollments. It includes most large universities in its membership and is the oldest existing athletic association. The NCAA's membership continues to grow, with incentives such as television revenues estimated at $370,000,000 for the 2002–03 fiscal year, including proceeds from a long-term contract with CBS amounting to several billion dollars (Fulks, 2002a). These revenues help fund participation in postseason championships and campus-based programs and provide membership incentives unmatched by the NAIA.

The NCAA dominates the governance of college sports based on its membership size, its early governance of the largest and most visible football programs, and its resources to support a large staff and infrastructure. NCAA rules and structures have become models for other associations. Its dominance was solidified beginning in the 1950s with the appointment of a full-time executive director, control of television rights, national tournaments, rules enforcement, and governance of postseason football bowl games (Tow, 1982).

The NCAA increasingly shares this dominance with affiliated conferences of colleges and universities that provide competition venues, championship opportunities, media contracts, access to NCAA tournaments, institutional identity, and access to the lucrative football Bowl Championship Series for some (Lombardi and others, 2003; Suggs, 2003b). The 1984 Supreme Court decision (*NCAA v. Board of Regents of the University of Oklahoma,* 1984) finding the NCAA in violation of antitrust laws in its control of college football television contracts occurred as cable television created a proliferation of new stations seeking programming opportunities. With the increased access to media markets and the related role in marketing their respective institutions, the conferences quickly gained heightened influence over the next fifteen years.

TABLE 1
Comparison of Key National Athletic Governing Associations

	National Collegiate Athletic Association (NCAA)	*National Association of Intercollegiate Athletics[a] (NAIA)*	*National Junior College Athletic Association[a] (NJCAA)*
Founding year and year women's programs added	Men: 1906 Women: 1983	Men: 1940 (as National Association for Intercollegiate Basketball), 1952 as NAIA; added women in 1980	Men: 1938 Women: 1975
Circumstances of origin	1906 response to White House, public, and institutional concerns regarding football excesses under leadership of President MacCracken, NYU, as the Intercollegiate Athletic Association of the United States; renamed NCAA in 1910	Inspired by concept of a small college basketball tournament in Kansas 1938, founded as National Association of Intercollegiate Basketball; founders included James Naismith, originator of basketball; became NAIA in 1952	Western community colleges seeking venue for sports competition
Purpose	"To maintain intercollegiate athletics as an integral part of the educational program and the athlete as an integral part of the student body, and by so doing, retain a clear line of demarcation between intercollegiate athletics and professional sports"[a]	"To promote the education and development of students through intercollegiate athletic participation. Member institutions . . . share a common commitment to high standards and the principle that athletics serve as an integral part of education"[b] (in practice aimed toward small colleges)	"To promote and foster junior college athletics on intersectional and national levels so that results will be consistent with the total educational program of its members"[c]

Recent approximate membership	Total: 1028 institutions (117 Division I-A, 1118 Division I-AA, 91 Division I-AAA, 281 Division II, 421 Division III)[d]	Total: 299 institutions[e]	Total: 358 institutions[f]
Structure	Three divisions based on institutional enrollment, athletic budgets and facilities: I, II, III, with Division I subdivided into three: I-A, I-AA, I-AAA	Fourteen geographic regions, basketball in two divisions	Three divisions by sport: I, II, III, Twenty-four geographic regions, California system eventually withdrew to be self-sufficient within state
Approximate number of student athletes	Total: 361,175[d] Women: 150,186; Men: 210,989 Division I: 148,614 Division II: 74,807 Division III: 137,754	63,169[h]	30,000[h]
Approximate annual budget	$370,000,000, 87 percent based in television revenues (2002–2003 fiscal year)	N/A	N/A

Notes: [a]NCAA, 2004a. [b]NAIA, n.d.a. [c]NJCAA, n.d.a. [d]NCAA, 2004d. [e]NAIA, 2004. [f]NJCAA, n.d.a. [g]NJCAA, n.d.b. [h]Calculated based on institutional total and averages for 2002–2003 (Suggs, 2004).

Suggs (2003a) describes the recent evolution and power of conferences as creating a new status hierarchy in the world of higher education extending beyond athletics.

The majority of student-athletes and the colleges and universities for which they compete are not the big-time sports institutions represented by NCAA Division I-A. The NCAA Division I-A, the most competitive and with the highest revenues, includes 117 of the 1,685 institutional members of the three associations in recent years as illustrated in Table 1. Within the NCAA alone, student-athletes from the full spectrum of Division I institutions represented fewer than half of the sports participants. Yet the conditions and concerns related to Division I men's football and basketball have had the greatest influence on the overall governance of college sports and the public's perception of them. Thus the perceptions affecting campus-based decision making related to athletics may typically represent the images or the schema associated with Division I sports though they do not represent a given campus's reality.

NCAA's Division I consists of 238 institutions engaging in programs serving both the campus and the community with a commitment to the highest level of competition in the spectator-oriented, income-producing sports of football and basketball. The magnitude and funding of these larger university programs distinguish the NCAA from other associations, which are primarily composed of colleges. In fiscal year 2001, the average athletics expenditure budget for Division I-A institutions with football was $23,200,000 (Fulks, 2002a). Division I-AA, Division I-AAA, Division II, and Division III had considerably lower average expenditure budgets at $6,800,000; $5,500,000; $2,300,000; and $1,248,000, respectively. Only Division I-A institutions reflected balanced budgets, on average, when institutional support was considered (Fulks, 2002a). Division I-AA and Division II athletics programs ran average deficits of $1.2 million in Division I-AA and about $400,000 each in Division I-AAA and Division II. The average deficits were one to two million dollars higher when institutional support was not considered in the equation (Fulks, 2002a, 2002b).

NCAA reports do not aggregate Division III revenues and expenses in the same way that they do those of Divisions I and II. However, the detailed tables of averages by sport across the division reveal a similar pattern of deficit spending. That the athletics arm race influences the Division III level is demonstrated by the 25 percent average increase in athletics expenditures across its 411 institutions between 1999 and 2001. This is the highest increase across NCAA divisions with the exception of the slightly higher 26 percent increase for Division I-AA expenditures (Fulks, 2002a, 2002b). To provide a sense of magnitude, the average deficit for a Division I-AA institution is nearly equivalent to the total average athletics budget for Division III colleges. At the same time, the athletics budgets of Division III may represent a higher proportion of the institutional budgets for the much smaller colleges and universities it represents than for the universities represented in Division I. This suggestion echoes the observations made in the Mellon Foundation studies about the relative impact of athletics on the culture of small institutions at which the numbers of student-athletes represent a much higher proportion of the student body than at large universities (Shulman and Bowen, 2001). Thus the issues related to Division III athletics are perhaps less sensational than those in the highly visible Division I, but they are comparable in concerns for cultural and financial impact.

The NAIA, consisting of approximately 299 small colleges in 2004, continues to face decreasing membership in competition with the wealthier NCAA, where the NAIA competes with Division III institutions for members. NCAA Division III numbered 421 active institutions in fall 2002.

The NJCAA, restricted to two-year colleges, is not faced with NCAA competition; indeed, it lists the NCAA as an affiliate. Nevertheless, the NJCAA has also decreased in size since the 1970s with its membership of about 550 institutions dropping to 358 listed members in 2004. With the diversity of associations and divisions within the associations, we will most frequently address NCAA Division I because of the influential role it plays in creating models and shaping values, often based on more commercialized programs, that have been adapted and adopted at all levels of college sports. This visibility has also led to a greater focus on Division I issues and institutions in the literature.

It is important to note too the powerful role of regional conferences such as the Southeastern Athletic Conference, the Ivy League, the Big Ten Conference, the Pacific 10, and the Patriot League in the governance, culture, economics, and marketing of college sports. Each has its own culture, resources, and governance and, in turn, represents a coalition of institutions in regard to NCAA decision making.

A full understanding of the contemporary structure of intercollegiate athletics requires some understanding of the historical dynamics that produced today's system. This view is tempered further by Stinchcombe's research (1965) suggesting that founding conditions influence the institutions they produce far into the future. Thus the following section provides a brief overview of that context as it relates to the major governing organizations of intercollegiate sports.

Historical Context: Men, Women, Football, and University Growth

Modern college sports were born after the Civil War, in the flush of the industrial revolution and the related developing transportation infrastructure. As the modern university blossomed and access to higher education increasingly democratized, men's sports became central to building attention and loyalty within an otherwise indifferent public (Chu, 1989; Rudolph, 1962, 1990; Sack and Staurowsky, 1998). The various student-initiated men's athletic associations in the midnineteenth century provided the first sustained occasion for collaboration among colleges and universities in the United States (Rudolph, 1962, 1990).

During this era, the doors of higher education began to open to women and African Americans in both segregated institutions and within some traditionally white and male colleges and universities. As student-organized men's sports became foundational to these institutions, women faculty sought a model for women's college sports that would avoid the abuses already plaguing men's sports (Festle, 1996; Kane, 2001; Oglesby, 2001). College sports for African American men in the era of Southern segregation became available in black colleges and universities, typically competing in conferences of like institutions. Beyond these early separate conferences, race did not play a role in the formal structure of college sports. However, student-athletes of color played an increasingly important role as participants in college sports over time. Race continues to play a role in the social and cultural context of sport (as we will discuss at greater length in a later chapter). The differential development of men's and women's sports influenced the underlying governing structure of today's intercollegiate sports.

Origins of Men's Sports: Student Initiated

The earliest efforts by students to organize men's college sports in the midnineteenth century originated with young men seeking competition opportunities, agreement on the rules of play, and some level of agreement over who was eligible to play (Stern, 1979; Hardy and Berryman, 1982; Chu, 1989). Thus there was little initial oversight until participants agreed on the need for some common rules. Students founded the first association governing multiple sports, the Intercollegiate Association of Amateur Athletics of America, in 1876. In the same year, students from Columbia, Harvard, and Princeton founded the Intercollegiate Football Association (Hardy and Berryman, 1982).

Problems quickly became associated with student-run men's sports programs including excesses in recruiting and other activities associated with sports, as well as apparent lack of control and inconsistent management of men's sports by transient student groups. Football was the largest, most costly, most visible, and most violent of the programs. Alumni soon became involved to provide longer-term stability. Faculty perceived the growing athletics enterprise as a threat to the academic integrity of colleges and universities. As a result, numbers of faculty became engaged in the governance of sports programs on campus beginning in the 1870s with hopes of bringing greater control and academic accountability to the enterprise. The Big Ten Conference, consisting of the largest institutions in the Midwest, was the first of several conferences formed by faculty rather than students.

Sustaining football required more than student initiative and faculty oversight, however, because stadiums required responsible financial management with substantial capital investments and management of resulting revenues and public visibility. Thus as football emerged as a popular link between an enamored public and college campuses seeking public support in the 1890s, administrations became more consistently involved in managing intercollegiate sports programs. However, this involvement developed after a pattern of excess had already been established.

If the context at the time of their founding largely shapes organizations over time, as Stinchcombe (1965) suggests, football shaped the NCAA. At the start of the twentieth century, football was relatively unregulated and poorly equipped. Injuries and deaths on collegiate gridirons, eighteen in 1905 alone, resulted in public outrage. Yet football captured the U.S. imagination unlike any other collegiate institution up to that time. The origin of New York's annual Thanksgiving Day parade around the annual Princeton-Yale football game symbolizes the cultural influence of football at the turn of the twentieth century. The Intercollegiate Athletic Association of the United States (IAAUS), the organization that would become the NCAA, was founded as a result of meetings and discussions following a White House summit in 1905. The summit called for football reform and reflected a desire to assure the survival of a popular cultural icon.

Ambitious to govern all collegiate sport, the initial goal of the IAAUS was "the regulation and supervision of college athletics throughout the United States in order that the athletic activities in the colleges and universities may be maintained on an ethical plane in keeping with the dignity and high purposes of education" (IAAUS Proceedings, 1906, p. 29, as cited in Frey, 1982, p. 22). By the time this national governing body was founded, football was already characterized by recruitment, incentives to athletes to play including scholarships, high gate receipts, significant spending on facilities, enthusiastic fan support, intense rivalries, full schedules, and identification with institutions for their football teams rather than their academic programs. This preexisting culture shaped and challenged the development of a system of rules attempting to assure fair competition and a commitment to amateurism in college sports embodied in the mission of the IAAUS and the ensuing NCAA. Although it was committed to the governance of all sports, the excesses and culture of football was the driving force for rules that would extend across the range of sports (Sack and Staurowsky, 1998; Fleisher, Goff, and Tollison, 1992).

In summary, campus-level control of men's college sports evolved over time across a number of constituencies. Students initiated and coordinated initial competitions and structures in the nineteenth century. Alumni entered in response to the need for stability and to build on efforts they had begun as undergraduates. Administration stepped in when athletics' potential effect on enrollment, revenue, facilities, and control became apparent. Faculty entered the arena for academic control to keep sport within the mission of higher education (Hardy and Berryman, 1982).

Origins of Women's Sports: Faculty Initiated and Governed

The distinctive context of the post-Civil War era shaped the evolution of women's sports in a very different way from that of men's. Until the 1850s, higher education for women was relatively rare, as was encouragement of the physical activity and competition associated with organized sports. After the Civil War, increasing numbers of women gained access to higher education. The founding of colleges for women as well as a growing coeducation movement, especially in the larger midwestern and western state universities, provided new opportunities for women. Higher learning for women was, nevertheless, a novelty in a society that did not yet view women as fit to vote.

Women's sports originated in the nineteenth century through the initiative and oversight of faculty—primarily in physical education. Physical education was included in the curriculum of newly founded women's colleges to offset questions that male scholars and administrators raised about the physical capacity of women to do intellectual work (Rudolph, 1962, 1990; Solomon, 1985). Physical education programs served to demonstrate that women had the physical capacity to do intellectual work and built on the image of a mind-body connection popular at the time (Gerber, 1975; Smith, 2000; Solomon, 1985).

The 1899 founding of the women's basketball rules committee of the American Association for the Advancement of Physical Education led by Senda Berenson from the Smith College faculty set a path for women's athletics very different from that of men's. Designed to be integral to academic programs and to avoid the perceived excesses of men's sports, the women's rules were developed through the professional association of physical education faculty. They typically restricted travel, championships, and gate receipts, emphasizing the value of participation for its own sake rather than for competition or the pleasure of spectators (Chu, 1989; Sack and Staurowsky, 1998). This philosophy of restraint and control of the enterprise eventually led to the substitution of play days for intercollegiate competition at many institutions. These sporting events mixed any interested women students from several colleges in teams competing and socializing on a single day without prior organization or practice (Cahn, 1994). Play days emphasized democratic participation without direct competition between institutions (Wushanley, 2004). Women's sports were conducted with a view toward expected behavior for women of the time and designed to avoid the excesses apparent in men's sports (Sack and Staurowsky, 1998). Given the focus, visibility, and resources committed to men's sports and the governance and philosophy undergirding women's sports, the male-dominated college sports world at the turn of the century saw little threat or competition from women's programs.

Early in the twentieth century, however, the growth of women's sports began to be viewed as a potential threat to the dominance of men's sports organizations. As a result, the American Athletic Union unsuccessfully attempted to take over governance of women's sports in the 1920s. The attempt, however, helped solidify women's physical educators resolve to organize to protect women's control of women's physical education and sports. The resulting model remained nonthreatening to men's programs in terms of resources and visibility until the passage of Title IX in 1972. With Title IX on the horizon, women physical educators, in response to their students' demands, departed from the physical education model and committed to competitive intercollegiate athletics for women by creating a national governing body for women's programs, the AIAW. Even as the AIAW was growing in size and visibility, the NCAA, led by Walters Byers, successfully took over the governance of women's sports in its member institutions where responses to Title IX and budgetary constraints were already combining previously separate men's and women's athletics departments (Festle, 1996; Hult, 1999; Sack and Staurowsky, 1998; Wu, 1999). Until the initial proposals for Title IX in the late 1960s, women's sports remained neglected by the institutions sponsoring them and unrecognized in national discussions of organized sport outside the organizations of women's physical educators (Hardy and Berryman, 1982).

The National Collegiate Athletic Association

The enthusiasm generated by intercollegiate football produced a mass following for the sport, as well as for individual teams, players, female cheerleaders, bands, and the colleges and universities with which they were identified. The most ambitious institutions at the advent of the twentieth century built large stadiums to enhance game attendance, gate receipts, and the anticipated enrollments that visibility would bring (Sack and Staurowsky, 1998; Chu, 1989; Hardy and Berryman, 1982).

In the years leading to the twentieth century, football caught campuses and communities by storm at a time when campuses faced threats to their sense of community as they grew in size and missions. In the context of this growth, football provided loyalty-building symbols and rituals (Toma, 1999; Chu, 1989). Campuses grew more vulnerable to the pageant of football as a result of (1) faculty members increasingly focused on classroom teaching, research, and scholarship rather than the whole life of students including extracurricular activities; (2) an evolving economy that provided leisure time for increasing numbers of people; (3) mass spectator sports, with football one of the most popular, providing a common focus for an increasingly diverse national population growing through immigration from countries and cultures throughout the world; (4) college and university presidents being pressured to sustain growing programs by attracting tuition-paying students, private philanthropy, and legislative support; and (5) a national can-do culture with limited understanding or interest in the new university's academic mission (Veysey, 1965; Henry, 1975; Chu, 1989).

Presidents found football a perfect vehicle for rallying the legions of students and members of the public around institutions with which they might not otherwise connect. The expectation was that the accompanying visibility would increase the resource flow to the institutions through enrollments, philanthropic giving, and legislative subsidies (Hardy and Berryman, 1982; Rudolph, 1962, 1990; Toma, 2003). Whether these effects were real or not, they became embedded in belief systems about the effects of athletics on institutional support.

By the turn of the twentieth century, college football, more than any other sport, already had an extensive list of stakeholders: students, athletes, coaches, athletics directors or managers, presidents, alumni, boards of trustees, faculty, the media, communities benefiting from the economic rewards of large football crowds, the college football association, and a public hungry for sports. Football also had its institutional critics, who viewed the excesses of sports as bad for both campus and society. College football was characterized by numerous abuses, including players recruited solely to compete, often for different institutions year to year or even week to week; competition schedules leaving little time for academics; and most seriously, high numbers of injuries and deaths resulting from unregulated competition in a physically violent sport. Even as the mass fascination with college football grew, so did calls for its abolition or reform. By the early twentieth century, presidents of a number of large universities viewed the crowds coming to the campus and following teams in the media as a source of public support for the new universities, whose academic missions the public neither clearly understood nor necessarily valued. Teams played several games a week with little of today's regulation or physical protection. As a result, students were routinely injured and even killed in collegiate football games. In a time of muckraking journalists and a public in the throes of the progressive era, demands grew for the elimination or reform of college football. In October 1905, after the deaths of eighteen football players on college gridirons across the country in a single year, President Theodore Roosevelt intervened.

With his own son on the Harvard football team, Roosevelt called a meeting of athletics representatives from Harvard, Princeton, and Yale to discuss the state of collegiate football. Accounts of his motivations vary from demanding reform or abolition to a fear of the loss of the popular and "manly" game in the face of rising demands for its abolition (Fleisher, Goff, and Tollison, 1992; Rudolph, 1962, 1990; Thelin, 1994; Sack and Staurowsky, 1998; Toma, 2003). Regardless of Roosevelt's motivation, the meeting produced a commitment to reduce the violence with rules changes. When the expected outcomes from this meeting failed to materialize, NYU Chancellor Henry MacCracken gathered a group of college presidents and athletics administrators to found the IAAUS with thirty-eight members in 1906 (Fleisher, Goff, and Tollison, 1992). Renamed the National Collegiate Athletic Association (NCAA) in 1910, it continued its commitment to amateurism in college sport competition as it grew over the years.

Rooted in football, the NCAA was born in the progressive era that was associated with rising professionalism, social reform, and the growth of large organizations (Rudolph, 1962, 1990; Veysey, 1965). Its founding marked the growing professionalizing of both university and athletics administration. The NCAA offered a professional identity and an association for a growing corps of athletics professionals employed within the country's largest, most prestigious institutions.

From the outset, the universities creating the NCAA faced several campus concerns around sports: (1) a growing distance between men's athletics and academic programs, (2) ongoing pressures toward commercialization, (3) challenges to amateurism, (4) the challenge of rising athletics costs, and (5) perceived threats to academic integrity.

The circumstances of the NCAA's founding centered on perceived abuses in football. The founding principles were based on a commitment to amateurism involving the student educational experience and participation without pay. Over time, in the quest for winning seasons, both institutions and coaches found it tempting to ignore these principles. Continuing cycles of scandal and reform in collegiate sports culminated in 1947 in a proposed NCAA *Sanity Code* (approved in 1948), entitled "Principles of Conduct of Intercollegiate Athletics," which was designed as a compromise in the ongoing debate about offering athletics financial aid (Fleisher, Goff, and Tollison, 1992). The short-lived code allowed student-athletes to accept need-based financial aid but with limits to tuition and incidental expenses. It also permitted off-campus recruiting (Sack and Staurowsky, 1998).

Depending on one's point of view, the sanity code either opened the floodgates to professionalizing college sports or acknowledged and put constraints on existing practices. Most important, perhaps, it defined a formal compliance role for the NCAA to enforce its constitutional provisions. Member institutions hoped that a central authority would stem the pattern of abuses that institutional self-regulation had failed to control. The sanity code was rescinded after two years because southern conferences rebelled against its constraints and threatened to withdraw from the NCAA. However, the compliance role of the NCAA emerged soon after; and the advent of a new media technology, television, would significantly change the NCAA's relationship to institutional athletics programs and the stakes involved in campus decision making. The acceptance of formal compliance systems and the ability to contract with television to broadcast college football games began to elevate the NCAA to the dominant national athletics association in the early 1950s.

Between 1951 and the 1984 Supreme Court decision outlawing the practice (*NCAA v. Board of Regents of the University of Oklahoma,* 1984), the NCAA held a virtual monopoly over contracts for televising collegiate athletic events. The resulting revenues, regulations, and visibility of NCAA-governed programs marked the ascendancy of the NCAA even in basketball, where the NAIA-sponsored National Invitational Tournament (NIT) had been comparable in the national eye to the NCAA tournament (Fleisher, Goff, and Tollison, 1992). By 2004, the proliferation of television stations contracting with individual institutions did not seem to threaten the continued filling of NCAA coffers as a function of multibillion-dollar contracts for televising NCAA-sponsored championships, highlighted by the basketball Final Four.

Over the course of the twentieth century, the NCAA became the dominant association governing college athletics, especially among the country's largest institutions. By 2002, the voluntary association of over one thousand colleges and universities governed intercollegiate athletics competition in over fifty sports for both men and women. Its roots are reflected in a governance structure that accords the greatest influence to Division I-A institutions with large football programs (programs using stadiums seating at least thirty thousand, an average attendance of seventeen thousand spectators, and an annual minimum athletics financial aid commitment exceeding a million dollars) (NCAA, 2004a).

The NCAA constitution provides the framework and defines limits for the group's governance, regulations, and purpose. Its fundamental policy addresses the following areas: (1) the principle of amateurism to assure athletics as an integral part of the educational program and (2) the athlete as an integral part of the student body establishing a "clear line of demarcation between intercollegiate athletics and professional sports" (NCAA, 2004a, p. 1). It further defines the individual and collective responsibilities of member institutions to apply and enforce legislation to assure competitive equity including "basic athletics issues such as admissions, financial aid, eligibility and recruiting" (p. 1).

Subsequent articles in the constitution also address the conduct of intercollegiate athletics, membership, organizational structure, legislative authority and process, and institutional control of intercollegiate athletics.

The NCAA constitution designates the chief executive officer of the institution, rather than the athletics director, as ultimately responsible for the conduct of the intercollegiate athletics program and the actions of any board in control of that program (NCAA, 2004a). Budgetary control of athletics programs falls within the realm of normal institutional budgetary procedures. Members conduct a self-study and analysis, modeled after academic accreditation processes, as part of an athletics certification process. This was instituted in the 1990s as recommended by the Knight Foundation Commission on Intercollegiate Athletics (1991) to study and propose reforms for college sports. The constitution also spells out the institution's responsibility for the acts of its staff members and any other individuals or agencies promoting the interests of the institution's intercollegiate athletics program.

The National Association of Intercollegiate Athletics (NAIA)

The NAIA grew from smaller, midwestern institutions and the sport of men's basketball. Although formally organized in 1940 at a hotel in Kansas City, Missouri, as the National Intercollegiate Basketball Association, its genesis lay in a 1937 men's basketball tournament in Kansas City's Municipal Auditorium, a tournament organized by a group of mostly local business leaders and Dr. James Naismith, originator of the game of basketball. The group's intent was "to provide Kansas City-area fans with exciting amateur competition and to provide a framework for small colleges and universities to determine a national basketball champion." The NAIA's philosophy and practice is committed to "academic achievement over athletic excellence," equal opportunity for all student-athletes, and "an expectation of ethical behavior and a commitment to scholarship, sportsmanship and leadership" (NAIA, n.d., n.p.). By the 1980s, the NAIA had grown to a national association governing athletics in a full range of sports in over five hundred small colleges. About 90 percent of NAIA institutions offer athletics scholarships (NAIA, n.d.).

The NAIA's membership has dropped from 474 institutions in 1988 to 299 by fall 2004 (NAIA, n.d.). The *Chronicle of Higher Education* (Blum,

1995a) cites several reasons for this pattern. They include the perceived financial benefits associated with NCAA membership, greater national media exposure, increased ability to draw valued recruits and donors associated with the NCAA, and the domino effect created when nearby institutions leave the NAIA for the NCAA.

Although not beset with the sporadic patterns of scandal associated with NCAA athletics, the NAIA followed compliance and reform efforts that the NCAA initiated. For example, it adopted NCAA-like rules and compliance procedures and increased leadership responsibility for presidents in the association shortly after the NCAA's similar restructuring to empower presidents. Unlike NCAA Division III, the NAIA permits the use of athletics scholarships in recruiting student-athletes.

The National Junior College Athletic Association (NJCAA)

The NJCAA originated in Fresno, California, to develop a national program of college sports for and consistent with the educational mission of junior colleges. Chartered in 1938, it was initially dominated by California community colleges, which have subsequently formed their own statewide association. Initial sports competition focused primarily on men's track and field. The NJCAA added men's basketball after World War II, with additional sports following. The NJCAA was a leader in strengthening college sports as an institution by creating affiliations with other organizations. Thus in 1957, it affiliated with the National Federation of High School Athletic Associations and the NAIA in a triumvirate called the National Alliance, which collaborated on developing common playing rules in football, six-man football, soccer, basketball, and other sports. After passage of Title IX in 1972, the NJCAA was the first of the national associations for men's athletics to include women in 1975 (NJCAA, n.d.b).

The Association of Intercollegiate Athletics for Women (AIAW)

Rooted in women's physical education departments, with an emphasis on education and cooperation, women's competitions were typically organized by women's coaches (who were primarily faculty members) making arrangements with their counterparts elsewhere. They used game rules formulated by individual membership professional associations of physical educators. In some cases, to avoid the evils of competition, players from competing schools were split into two teams, each with players from both schools. However, by the 1960s, reflecting the growing women's movement and with Title IX on the horizon, women students sought high-caliber competition to provide championship opportunities. Demands of students for gender equity in athletics led to the creation of the AIAW. Active during the 1970s, at its peak the AIAW regulated at least forty-two thousand teams and sponsored forty-one championships in nineteen sports (Festle, 1996; Hult, 1999; Slatton, 1982).

The AIAW, then the dominant association governing women's intercollegiate sports, met its demise in 1982, when the NCAA and the NAIA committed to sponsoring women's championships. The NCAA appealed to male-dominated university and athletics administrations by providing the economy of paying dues to only one association for their increasingly consolidated men's and women's programs. Further, the NCAA offered financial incentives and media guarantees for championship participation. Consolidation of men's and women's athletics departments made a single governing association both simple and workable. The administrators of the combined athletics programs were, for the most part, men familiar with the structure, functioning, and values of the NCAA. The AIAW's fate was sealed when it committed rapidly dwindling resources to unsuccessful legal action against the NCAA (Festle, 1996; Hult, 1999; Wushanley, 2004).

After the AIAW's demise in 1982, women's athletics at the institutional level continued to be folded into the dominant men's programs. Their governance fell under the national associations dominated by a more commercial and competitive male model of athletics. Women who had been leaders within their campus and national associations were subordinated to male administrators. Similarly, the coaching of women's teams began a transition from female coaches to a trend toward men coaching women's teams, despite the obvious success of women coaches. A number of analysts of the AIAW and Title IX note the disempowering effect of Title IX on women's governance of women's sports given an imbalance of power in the sports arena (Sack and Staurowsky, 1998; Kane, 2001; Festle, 1996). Combined with the effects of media contracts and the economy of football in relation to men's sports, the demise of the student- and curriculum-centered AIAW was a major step in the growing dominance of the NCAA in the arena of college sports.

The Power and Influence of Regional Conferences

Before the evolution of national associations, regional conferences or leagues provided collaborative venues for competition and rules. The faculty-governed Big Ten Conference was one of the first and most enduring of the major athletics conferences. But the Southeastern Conference and the Ivy League share roots nearly as deep. The conferences are key forces in the governance of intercollegiate athletics representing coalitions of institutions within the NCAA. As a later chapter will discuss, the conference structure has ascended in power with the 1984 Supreme Court decision against the NCAA monopoly over television rights in college sports (*NCAA v. Board of Regents of the University of Oklahoma,* 1984) and the more recent creation of the Bowl Championship Series (BCS) in football (Suggs, 2003a, 2003b). The BCS has triggered a high-stakes reshuffling of conference memberships as those institutions in conferences that are not automatically eligible for the BCS and the financial rewards associated with it jockey for inclusion in conferences that are.

Dilemmas and Tensions Revealed by a Structural View

Competition demands collaboration, yet collaboration means compromising campus autonomy. The professionalized infrastructure of the NCAA places a sports-oriented culture at the hub of that collaboration daily. The training, priorities, and experience of athletics professionals informs a view of the campus through a window in the gym rather than one in the campus library. In constructing an understanding of the university, the athletics department is likely to see the institution very differently from an academic administrator. The decisions and practices that the NCAA implements with the guidance of athletics professionals have implications within the campus's academic culture. NCAA high school course requirements, minimum academic requirements for eligibility on admission, and standards for satisfactory academic progress are examples of NCAA requirements affecting the academic experience of students at the campus level. A myriad of athletics professions and professional associations helps shape the worldview of campus staff in athletics. As a result, we might see an eroding institutional identification as personnel identify with the profession and migrate over the course of a career from one institution to another. That experience provides breadth and depth in the athletics enterprise but limited exposure to the college or university as an academic organization.

The interests of institutions with large football programs and large stadiums to support them have heavily influenced NCAA structure, regulations, decision-making processes, and procedures. Regulations and structures designed to reform excesses primarily in Division I football have been replicated among other divisions within the NCAA, in the NAIA, and in the NJCAA. Absent the kinds of problems triggering the structure of rules and decision making within the NCAA Division I-A, this evolution makes little sense on the surface. However, the NCAA Division III, the NJCAA, and the NAIA's pattern of adopting NCAA-like processes is consistent with the concept of mimetic isomorphism (Powell and DiMaggio, 1991), in which organizations strive to enhance their own status by mimicking more prestigious peers. These replication processes explain, in the case of college sports dominated numerically by small institutions, a structure of rules responsive to perceived abuses in Division I revenue-producing sports. Smaller programs, far greater in number, chafe under a structure less applicable to their missions and structures.

Finally, institutional and NCAA practices have resulted in the loss of women's control over women's athletics on campus and in the loss of a national governance model for women. Each of these increments was at least partially a result of the passage of Title IX. The cultural and economic forces leading to the failure of women's attempts to govern women's sports nationally affected the on-campus structure of women's sports. Very quickly, the male-dominated model filtered down to presidents and athletics directors actively seeking ways to reduce spending. Title IX represents one of a range of external laws and regulations that influence campus decision making and culture related to athletics. The next chapter will explore these issues in greater depth.

The Legal and Regulatory Context

CONSISTENT WITH ITS COMMITMENT to the letter and spirit of the Americans with Disabilities Act (ADA), State University has admitted a student with a math learning disability. The otherwise high-achieving student received accommodation in high school with a combination of individual tutoring and a special math course that was not part of the college preparation curriculum. As an all-state quarterback, the student was also recruited to play football at State U. Math is not required for his social work major, and the math and science requirements will allow him to complete his course of study with a combination of lab sciences, requiring no accommodation for his disability beyond the waiver of the college-track math course in the application process. Because he did not complete the course that the National Collegiate Athletics Association (NCAA) requires for eligibility, he is declared ineligible for competing on the football team. He threatens to sue State U. and the NCAA for discrimination under the ADA. The NCAA responds that it is not accountable to the ADA because it is not a covered enterprise.

This scenario shows the university at the intersection of three sets of rules: the NCAA's rules, State U.'s academic norms and policies, and state and federal laws. Rules and regulations provide structure and pathways for the relationships between a college or university and the organizations and agencies constituting its environment. Related to higher education and athletics, these include rules of athletics-governing associations with which the college or university affiliates, federal and state statutes and regulations, and interpretations of statutes and rules through the courts and association compliance groups, respectively. Intercollegiate athletics illustrate the complexity resulting when organizations dwell within multiple social institutions, which "exist, overlap, and offer competitive formulation and prescriptions" (Scott, 2001, p. 208).

This chapter examines the context for university decision making and leadership related to athletics as defined by rules embodied in internal processes, federal and state law and regulation, the courts, and the regulations of national associations such as the NCAA. This literature review emphasizes both the intended and unintended effects of processes associated with the legal and regulatory context of the college or university. Given the long-term impact of conditions on the founding of institutions (Stinchcombe, 1965), we begin with a brief review of historical background related to the origins of legal and quasi-legal regulation of intercollegiate sports and their institutional sponsorship.

Origins and Impact of Rules

Consistent with the concept of judicial deference to academic expertise, both courts and legislatures traditionally respected a doctrine of autonomous self-regulation in colleges and universities up until the 1960s (Hobbs, 1981; Kaplin and Lee, 1995). However, since then higher education has become fully subject to the culture of litigation increasingly characterizing U.S. society (Gouldner, 1980). Externally, statutes and torts claims have imposed constraints and risks for postsecondary institutions to manage. Within higher education, college sports have provided fertile ground for building a complex structure of rules to govern intercollegiate competition and formal legal action to monitor or regulate abuses.

Historical Context

Men's sports were the first subjected to attempted regulation of college athletics beginning in the nineteenth and early twentieth centuries. The evolution of the NCAA as an organization shaped by the effort to control college football and later basketball largely influenced the nature and structure of rules for recruiting, eligibility, competition, and governance. In turn, these NCAA Division I rules and structures shaped those both at less commercialized NCAA levels and in other governing associations.

Women's sports, with different origins than men's sports, remained outside the reach and interest of both the NCAA and other associations and college administrations for nearly a century. At their inception in the nineteenth century, the educational model of women's sports placed its governance with faculty in physical education. The programs were thus beyond the perceived need for the elaborate systems of rules evolving in the attempt to control men's sports. As we discussed earlier, the formal regulation of men's sports was deeply responsive to abuses in football. Women's sports, however, was embedded in an entirely different tradition, an educational model, remaining separate and generally unattended to by college administrators and the NCAA until the 1980s.

Colleges intentionally embedded women's sports in the curriculum to create a model different from men's sports. Women's rules were developed through professional associations in which physical education faculty participated as individuals (Hardy and Berryman, 1982; Sojka, 1985). Football, in contrast, and later other men's sports, were governed and perceived as institutional activities with rules made through national institutional membership organizations. Essentially, until the advent of Title IX in the 1970s, men's and women's sports literally and metaphorically lived in different sections of the college or university, in vastly different quarters, under different supervision, and with windows opening to very different environments. Men's programs were in the front and highly visible, women in a small space in the back, invisible to the public and much of the institution. Men's programs eventually absorbed women's intercollegiate athletics, creating single departments. At the same time, beginning in the early 1980s, the NCAA and other smaller associations took over the governance of women's sports. This takeover combined in impact with NCAA decisions in the early 1950s to manage media contracts and to grant control formally to the association through rule making and sanctions for its membership (Stern, 1979), resulting in the NCAA's central influence in making rules for both women's and men's sports. Other athletics associations, such as the National Junior College Athletic Association or the National Association for Intercollegiate Athletics (NAIA), focused less on rules and compliance, often borrowing models from the NCAA. Thus we will focus our attention related to voluntary regulation primarily on the NCAA.

NCAA Regulations

A rich literature documents the evolution of men's intercollegiate athletics, the NCAA, and the ongoing efforts to reform athletics. The literature describes recurring variations of the apparent abuses triggering the founding of the NCAA (Toma, 2003; Thelin, 1994; Thelin and Wiseman, 1989; Lucas and Smith, 1978; Sack and Staurowsky, 1998; Hardy and Berryman, 1982; Festle, 1996). As we described previously, persistent concerns in the century after the creation of football included rampant commercialism, the threat to the amateur athlete, an erosion of academic values associated with sports, unethical practices in the effort to generate winning teams and the hoped-for revenues associated with them, misconduct by student-athletes and coaches, and the later denial of opportunities for African Americans and women to participate in college sports.

Much as most of the issues sound similar to those triggering Roosevelt's call for reform in 1906, the specifics related to these issues evolved and changed. New regulations evolved to curb imaginative skirting of existing regulations. The regulations were generated originally for football, the single largest, most costly, and popular sport.

The governance structure and associated rules for the NCAA's three divisions are codified in the annually published *NCAA Manual* (NCAA, 2004a, 2004b, 2004c). The NCAA publishes the manual for the voluntary, unincorporated membership organization annually in hard copy and posts it online with up to four revisions during a given year. At its heart is the NCAA constitution and the two-part fundamental policy addressing (1) the principle of amateurism to assure athletics as an integral part of the educational program and the athlete as an integral part of the student body establishing a "clear line of demarcation between intercollegiate athletics and professional sports" (NCAA, 2004a, p. 1); and (2) the individual and collective responsibilities of member institutions to apply and enforce legislation to assure competitive equity including "basic athletics issues such as admissions, financial aid, eligibility and recruiting" (p. 1).

The NCAA rules are designed to prevent abuses of its basic principles. However, at nearly five hundred pages and with regulations governing everything from gambling to the timing and number of phone calls university personnel can make to high school recruits, the possibility for inadvertent violations is high. For example, the bylaw prescribing the conditions that prospective student-athletes must meet in order to be eligible to compete in NCAA-sanctioned athletic competition consists of thirty-seven pages of rules. In order to assist high schools and aspiring student-athletes, the NCAA established an initial eligibility clearinghouse to certify high school athletes' academic qualifications based on grades especially in designated courses and test scores. Sections beyond the constitution address the conduct of intercollegiate athletics, NCAA membership, organizational structure, legislative authority and process, and institutional control of intercollegiate athletics. The constitution designates the chief institution's executive officer (as opposed to its athletics director) as ultimately responsible "for the conduct of the intercollegiate athletics program and the actions of any board in control of that program" (NCAA, 2004a, p. 49). The increasing complexity of the NCAA regulations typically requires a campus to have professional oversight and interpretation in order to feel assured of its compliance.

In the year 2000, for example, the NCAA sanctioned twelve institutions for major infractions and processed 2,024 cases involving secondary infractions. In a given year, the NCAA may approve and implement two hundred rule changes. Such rapidly changing extensive regulation highlights the critical importance of having professionals on campus who are knowledgeable about the rules. The NCAA system of control, then, creates a self-perpetuating bureaucracy. A growing corps of personnel with a professional stake in a complex web of regulations acquires expertise at the campus, conference, and NCAA levels.

Although presidents of NCAA member institutions hold considerable influence over the organization, many other parties are involved in developing athletics-related regulations. The processes of rule making, dominated by NCAA staff, and enforcement, involving both NCAA and campus staff, create commitments of organizational resources to assure knowledge and compliance. Thus, most Division I athletics departments have at least one full-time staff person committed to NCAA compliance. Additional positions throughout the university are committed at least partially to athletics to assure institutional adherence to the letter and spirit of both NCAA and government regulations related to intercollegiate athletics. Areas such as student records, admissions, financial aid, academic affairs, and student affairs all represent offices and programs with a responsibility and associated staff committed to assuring that their policies, procedures, and in some cases students are in compliance with regulations. The commitments are on the margins but may well add up to significant hidden costs. Major violations of NCAA rules require the institution to investigate and submit recommendations for sanctions to the NCAA. Given the required expertise and the potential risks to public image in an investigation, many institutions will engage at considerable expense law firms, often staffed with former NCAA compliance officers, to conduct the investigation and work with the NCAA in identifying appropriate sanctions.

Statutory and Case Law

Campuses are sometimes caught at the intersection of the implications of federal laws, evolving case law, and conflicting NCAA rules. The complex and conflicting social and cultural forces producing the laws also challenge campus leadership and decision making.

In addition to NCAA regulations, statutory law such as Title IX, Title VI of the Civil Rights Act of 1964, and the ADA affect and constrain institutional policies and practices related to intercollegiate athletics. Further, court rulings and interpretations also affect and constrain institutions spanning issues from torts claims regarding catastrophic injury, Supreme Court rulings related to the rights of individual campuses to negotiate media contracts, and gender equity in athletics.

Beyond case law and administrative regulations, a web of federal and state statutes surrounds both university and athletics policies and practices. Some are highly visible and even contentious, such as Title IX of the Education Amendments of 1972, which prohibits discrimination based on gender. Others, including a variety of employment laws, are so embedded in institutional policy that they are virtually invisible. As such, ongoing interpretation and implementation is a function of specialized offices, each interacting through separate avenues with the external environment. We will address some that specifically help frame institutional decision making and intercollegiate sports. With the exception of Title IX, we will treat others more briefly to convey a sense of the volume and the differing ways in which they connect the institution and the external environment.

Employment Law Employment laws and policies include areas such as the Fair Labor Standards Act (defining areas requiring hourly or salaried compensation), the Occupational Safety and Health Act, immigration laws, the Family and Medical Leave Act, state and federal laws governing collective bargaining, and a number of laws prohibiting discrimination. Within a large institution, each of these might be the responsibility of a different office. An office of human resources, for example, might be responsible for assuring compliance with the Fair Labor Standards Act and the Family and Medical Leave Act, whereas an affirmative action office might be responsible for compliance with laws prohibiting discrimination. In turn, a facilities management department might be responsible for assuring compliance with the Occupational Safety and Health Act. Campus rules and expectations for compliance are incorporated in college- or university-wide procedures related to the various offices as exemplified by personnel search requirements. Institutionalization within various offices often masks both the external demands behind rule compliance and the different channels to outside agencies through which those offices interact.

Federal and Local Tax Law Tax codes have implications related to athletics programs and their role within the institution. Tax exemptions from local, state, and federal governments result from the status of college athletics programs as part of not-for-profit educational organizations. The land and facilities used for athletics programs are generally exempt from local property tax liability because these programs are part of their colleges and universities. Further, revenues associated with ticket sales and concessions are typically exempt from corporate income tax liability. The unrelated business income tax under the IRS code (26 U.S.C. §511–513) could impose tax liability if athletics activities such as ticket sales and concessions were viewed as being outside the university's educational function. Kaplin and Lee (1995) and Wong (1994) provide useful resources related to the full and complex range of tax implications for higher education and college sports ranging from tax exemption for student financial aid to unrelated business income tax. Tax liabilities represent areas in which athletics administrators and those in administrative areas such as business, finance, and human resources must be cognizant to assure institutional compliance.

Antitrust Law Through the Sherman Anti-Trust Act (1973) as well as state laws affecting both associations and conferences, both students and institutions have used the courts to sue based on alleged antitrust law violations by national associations, primarily the NCAA (Kaplin and Lee, 1995). Antitrust cases have, for example, affected the rules for distribution of the spoils associated with lucrative media contracts for athletic events, the conditions under which student-athletes might turn professional, and payment limits on assistant coaches.

From the advent of television until the Supreme Court intervened in the early 1980s, the NCAA regulated, contracted, and distributed revenues generated through televising intercollegiate athletic contests, especially football. The U.S. Supreme Court ended that practice in 1984 with the regulation and distribution of media revenues. *NCAA v. Board of Regents of the University of Oklahoma* (1984), won by the University of Oklahoma, joined by the University of Georgia, found that the NCAA television contract for college football games for 1982–1985 violated the Sherman Anti-Trust Act. As a result, the relationship between individual campuses and conferences and the media was deregulated, allowing bidding wars for the most prominent football and basketball games.

In relation to governance, two related cases, the *Association for Intercollegiate Athletics for Women v. NCAA* (1983, 1984), which the NCAA won in D.C. District Court, essentially sounded the death knell for the AIAW and its role as a separate governing agency for intercollegiate athletics for women. The NCAA had begun to move aggressively into the area of women's athletics, offering televised women's championships to institutions that were already members under their men's programs. When the broadcast competition from the NCAA threatened advertising profits for NBC's coverage of AIAW championships, NBC refused to honor its television contract with the AIAW. Unable to compete with the behemoth NCAA in the financial support of its own championships, the AIAW staked its financial future on winning the antitrust suit against the NCAA and lost on technicalities before reaching an antitrust hearing.

Antitrust laws have been used to challenge NCAA employment rules for both coaches and student-athletes. NCAA rules limiting the earnings of some assistant coaches were found to be a violation of antitrust laws (*Law v. NCAA,* 1998). Opponents of the structure of the football Bowl Championship Series threatened legal action under antitrust laws, alleging that the structure unfairly limits participation and rewards to a relatively small group of institutions (Suggs, 2003b).

Although few people may perceive the antitrust actions against the NCAA as affecting individual institutions, there are clear implications at the campus level. Antitrust actions aimed at the national association level generally occur several steps removed from individual institutions. Yet rulings in favor of institutions relative to television contracts, for example, benefit large, highly visible programs in large markets far more than they do smaller institutions in smaller markets.

Laws Prohibiting Discrimination A variety of state and federal laws have been enacted since the 1960s to prohibit discrimination based on race, ethnicity, disability, gender, religion, and other categories. The application of most of such laws to athletics was nullified in the *Grove City College v. Bell* decision of the U.S. Supreme Court in 1984, which held that Title IX (and by extension, comparable statutes) applied only to specific programs receiving federal funds rather than to the institution as a whole. The subsequent Civil Rights Restoration Act in 1989 clarified the intent of Congress that civil rights laws would apply to a full institution receiving federal funds through any of its programs. The institutional liability for violations of statutes such as Title VI of the Civil Rights Act of 1964 and Title IX of the Education Amendments of 1972 increased with *Franklin v. Gwinnett* (1991) in which the U.S. Supreme Court ruled that complainants could sue for monetary damages in Title IX cases. Prior to this ruling, an institution losing a Title IX lawsuit would be required to correct the situation but would not be levied financial damages. On the heels of the Civil Rights Restoration Act, this case increased the incentives for compliance with Title IX and similar statutes meant to assure nondiscrimination.

Like *Franklin v. Gwinnett* (1991), a number of court rulings have set precedents with the force of law in their interpretations of statutes. Several have shaped institutional conduct of intercollegiate athletics programs.

Title VI of the Civil Rights Act of 1964 prohibits discrimination based on race or color in the programs of covered institutions. A group of African American student-athletes who had been declared ineligible to compete for failure to meet the minimum required SAT score as required by NCAA Proposition 16 despite meeting NCAA minimum GPA requirements charged the NCAA with violations. The student-athletes prevailed in the district court. However, the Third Circuit Appeals Court reversed the decision, ruling that the NCAA was not a recipient of federal funds based solely on its relationship with member institutions and was therefore not covered under Title VI (1964).

The U.S. Supreme Court similarly found in *NCAA v. Smith* (1999) that a volleyball player alleging that the NCAA violated Title IX because of its rule affecting her institution could not prevail because the NCAA was an indirect recipient of federal funds and not covered by Title IX. The rulings illustrate the dilemma of member institutions that are responsible to the full range of civil rights laws when the NCAA is not. If a university functions under the rules of national associations that are not accountable to federal law, it may be in jeopardy for any violations of federal law occurring as a result of compliance with NCAA rules that might conflict. Rules that athletics professionals develop at the national level, without institutional oversight by those in other relevant professional arenas such as human resources, student affairs, or equal opportunity, can put the institution in a bind between NCAA rules and institutional accountability to laws to which the NCAA may not be subject.

A final example related to prohibiting discrimination applies to Section 504 of the Rehabilitation Act of 1973 and the ADA. Both statutes prohibit discrimination based on disability in employment and programs of educational institutions. The laws require the provision of reasonable accommodations to allow the full participation of qualified persons who have a disability. The vignette at the beginning of this chapter illustrates the concept of reasonable accommodation in allowing a substitution for a required course that was not central to the student's program of study. The accommodation, however, would have put the institution out of compliance with NCAA rules regarding required high school courses, illustrating the dilemma produced by a governing body at a distance from the enterprise it governs and lacking accountability under the same laws as member organizations.

Federal law as well as many state laws continue to avoid inclusion of sexual orientation or gender identity as a basis for civil rights protection. The NCAA has, however, added sexual orientation to its rules requiring member athletics programs not to discriminate on this basis.

Gender equity has become central to the intersection among intercollegiate athletics, the law, and societal values. Title IX of the Education Amendments of 1972, prohibiting discrimination based on sex in programs receiving federal funds, has been the object of scorn, celebration, confusion, frustration, and challenge in its application to intercollegiate athletics. Despite the diversity of views related to the nature of Title IX's impact, few would debate the magnitude of its effect.

Title IX: Prohibiting Gender Discrimination in Education

Given its actual and perceived impact on intercollegiate athletics within the past two decades, Title IX of the Education Amendments (1972) warrants separate treatment. On its surface, Title IX was simple: "No person in the United States shall, on the basis of sex, be excluded from participation in, be denied the benefits of, or be subjected to discrimination under any education program or activity receiving federal financial assistance."

A key victory on the part of the modern women's movement, Title IX sought to provide access to employment and educational opportunities in U.S. schools and colleges through constraints on receiving federal aid. For the first time, colleges and universities were required to remove quotas and limitations on the numbers of women admitted, for example, to law and medical schools. Though equity in athletics was not high on the agenda for advocates seeking the passage of Title IX in 1972, it was very much at the forefront for those involved in college sports and their national organizations, including Walter Byers, executive director of the NCAA, and members of the AIAW (Festle, 1996).

When Title IX was passed, its immediate effects on athletics were secondary to its effects on academic programs. Indeed, it was almost a decade before federal regulations governing the application and interpretation of Title IX relative to intercollegiate athletics were published in 1979 (Department of Health, Education, and Welfare, Office of Civil Rights, 1979). The developing regulations were subject to heated public discussion.

The regulations and subsequent policy interpretations specified thirteen factors for evaluating equity in athletics opportunities for the two sexes (Bonnette and Daniel, 1990):

- Athletics financial assistance
- Effective accommodation of interests and abilities of members of both sexes in selection of sports and levels of competition
- Provision of equipment and supplies
- Scheduling of games and practice time
- Travel and per diem allowance
- Opportunities for coaching and academic tutoring
- Assignment and compensation of coaches and tutors
- Provision of locker rooms, practice and competitive facilities
- Provision of medical and training facilities and services
- Provision of housing and dining facilities and services
- Publicity
- Support services
- Recruitment of student-athletes

The issues associated with the accommodation of interests and abilities and with athletics financial assistance have drawn the greatest initial attention in the courts, compliance agencies, and policy efforts. This attention perhaps reflects the primary issues associated with access for women to intercollegiate athletics. Without access, other issues were moot.

In 1984, only a year after institutions were expected to finish planning and comply with the law, the U.S. Supreme Court effectively declared the application of Title IX to athletics null in *Grove City College v. Bell* (1984). The Grove City decision relieved the pressure on college athletics departments to attend closely to the matter of gender equity while dealing with increased financial pressures associated with both NCAA compliance and campus budget priorities. In relation to athletics, federal rule making and compliance had come slowly, especially with the 1980 election of President Ronald Reagan, whose administration had an overt commitment to cut back enforcement of Title IX and narrow its interpretation (Festle, 1996). Campuses' failure to comply voluntarily with Title IX in their athletics programs left progress at a virtual standstill. The Grove City decision and antipathy by the executive branch responsible for Title IX enforcement abetted this failure.

The Civil Rights Restoration Act of 1987 (1988), enacted over the veto of President Reagan, once again provided a basis for federal suit for violation of Title IX as it applied to intercollegiate athletics. Distrust of both the commitment and capacity of the U.S. Office of Civil Rights to enforce Title IX led female student-athletes to the courts to assert their legal rights under Title IX and the Civil Rights Restoration Act. We can describe subsequent history, like the literature related to Title IX and gender equity in athletics, in terms of two discourses: advocacy and resistance, with a third, accommodation, quietly taking place at the campus level. Subsequent sections provide an overview of these themes with implications for decision making about campus athletics, institutional leadership, and campus culture.

Advocacy

Advocates for women's sports before and during enactment of Title IX were primarily the women physical educators who had served as stewards over the years. Male athletics administrators, campus leaders, and the educators' own professional associations virtually neglected their efforts, as did many in the feminist movement who viewed athletics as a male domain. Festle (1996) notes that anonymity served the women physical educators well in allowing them freedom to run women's athletics programs as they saw fit, creating an alternative to a male model of sports. From the perspective of women's sports advocates, enactment of Title IX brought some successes but also unintended consequences counter to women's control of their athletics programs and their fundamental values.

The women's movement and the debates leading to the enactment of Title IX in the late 1960s moved women physical educators out of anonymity and onto a political stage involving the NCAA, their own organization, feminist groups, and Congress. They organized, forming the Association for

Intercollegiate Athletics for Women (AIAW) to govern and offer championships in women's collegiate sports and were active partners in the National Coalition for Girls and Women in Education, formed in response to opposition to Title IX (Festle, 1996). By 1982, the AIAW held forty-one annual championships in nineteen different sports across three divisions. It regulated over forty-two thousand teams in its first nine years (Wushanley, 2004; Festle, 1996). According to Festle (p. 214), the organization valued caring about students, one another, and their processes with a commitment to creating an organization "that was fair, democratic, inclusive, conciliatory, and responsible. This attention to process, as well as their pioneering efforts to create a new model, resulted in an organization very different from the NCAA."

The success of the physical educators to both control women's sports and to provide an alternative to a male model was short-lived, however. Under the leadership of its executive director, Walter Byers, the NCAA aggressively sought to consolidate its dominance over college sports when it became clear that Title IX would pass and affect intercollegiate athletics. Even as the AIAW grew in size and influence during the 1970s, Byers worked with the NCAA and member institutions to initiate women's championships, beginning negotiations for television rights to Division I women's championships before the NCAA had officially proposed offering them. As noted previously, the combination of pressures from Title IX, fiscal pressures, and the NCAA's commitment to women's championships drove campuses to combine men's and women's athletics programs into a single department governed in practice by male administrators and with the competitive values of men's athletics. The AIAW began to dissolve in 1982, its fate sealed with the failure of its legal action against the NCAA in 1983 and 1984 (*AIAW v. NCAA,* 1983, 1984).

Women's participation in intercollegiate athletics blossomed as the opportunities that Title IX triggered opened up to them. Between the 1981–82 and 1998–99 academic years, the number of women's collegiate teams grew from 5,695 to 9,479, an increase of 66 percent. According to the Government Accounting Office (GAO, 2001), men's teams also increased in this period but at a much slower rate, from 9,113 to 9,149, an increase of 0.4 percent. Even as numbers of participation opportunities for women students increased, the numbers of women hired to coach them decreased in NCAA-sponsored programs from 90 percent in 1972 to 41.7 percent in 2004 (Acosta and Carpenter, 2004). Similarly, women became nearly invisible in athletics administration, from over 90 percent administrators of women's programs in 1972 to 8.1 percent, 16.9 percent, and 27.5 percent as athletics directors in combined NCAA Division I, Division II, and Division III programs, respectively, by 2004 (Acosta and Carpenter, 2004).

Increased participation opportunities and athletics financial aid for women did not come easily (Cahn, 1994; Guttman, 1991; Festle, 1996). In addition, advocacy by women professionals in the field and a series of lawsuits by women student-athletes in the early 1990s made it clear that institutions would be subject to legal action if they failed to comply with Title IX. The decision of the Supreme Court not to hear Brown University's appeal of the *Cohen v. Brown* decision (1995) upholding the U.S. Office of Civil Rights (OCR) Title IX guidelines affirmed the guidelines' authority. A 1997 class action suit related to gender equity in athletics financial aid by the National Women's Legal Fund with OCR against twenty-five universities in 1997 put a national spotlight on the slow pace of equity and accelerated progress toward equity (Naughton and Fiore, 1997).

The effect of Title IX on athletics more than thirty years after its passage remains mixed. Although women's participation is higher than most advocates had imagined at the outset, it came at a cost of subordination to an enterprise shaped by the values of large-scale men's athletics. It resulted in a reduction in opportunities for women's participation in coaching and athletics administration. Participation under the educational values that had previously characterized women's sports was also reduced. Compliance with Title IX highlights an arena in which the goals and perspectives of equity and fairness represent very different realities to different observers.

Resistance

Previous sections articulate the strong lobbying efforts in Congress against Title IX and its athletics regulations. Yet the bill passed, and its requirements became increasingly institutionalized. In athletics, however, active resistance has persisted.

The progress of women's participation in intercollegiate athletics is remarkable both in the strides women have made and in the depth of resistance over a third of a century. The NCAA, an organization committed solely to the governance of male athletics in the 1960s, actively fought enactment of Title IX and its later regulations related to athletics (Festle, 1996; Wushanley, 2004). Under Byers's leadership, the NCAA committed its considerable resources to lobbying Congress, building coalitions with higher education associations concerned with the potential costs of compliance, planning for its ultimate takeover of women's athletics, and supporting legal action that could undermine women's governance of women's sports and the application of Title IX to athletics (Festle, 1996; Wushanley, 2004).

The Civil Rights Restoration Act of 1987 was enacted in 1988 as institutions and athletics programs within them sought to meet the increased costs for NCAA membership and compliance. Rising tuition costs steadily increased the athletics budgets committed to financial aid. As institutions allocated resources to protect revenue-producing sports and to increase opportunities for women, resources for nonrevenue sports tended to drop (Fulks, 2002a, 2002b). Court cases such as *Cohen v. Brown* (1995) served notice that cutting women's teams was legally risky. Thus, despite their small budgets, men's Olympic sports, those neither attracting nor seeking paid spectators, tended to become targets for reduction in many institutions. A number of lawsuits by male student-athletes challenged the elimination of men's teams as sex discrimination under Title IX, and the OCR rulings supported Title IX and its regulations against constitutional challenges in at least eight federal circuit courts (*National Wrestling Association v. U.S. Department of Education,* 2003).

Despite clear evidence to the contrary in reports, research, and court rulings (NCAA, 2002; GAO, 2001; Acosta and Carpenter, 2004; *National Wrestling Coaches v. U.S. Department of Education,* 2003), media and plaintiff lawyers continue to reinforce a prevailing belief that Title IX has caused a reduction in men's opportunities to participate in athletics. There has certainly been a redistribution of those opportunities with larger football rosters and a small reduction in the absolute numbers of men's teams. Overall, the NCAA reports an increase of male participants in NCAA member programs from 167,055 to 209,890 from academic year 1981–82 to 2001–02 (NCAA, 2003a). Thelin (2000) closely analyzes the timing of rules changes that contributed to escalated spending in college sports and the application of Title IX after the greatest escalation had occurred. The escalation occurring when Title IX was effectively suspended raised the ante required for an institution to compete within the NCAA once the Civil Rights Restoration Act of 1987 reinstated Title IX. There appeared to be little consideration of achieving equity by restoring men's sports to earlier levels of funding.

Women's Accommodation to a Male Model

Despite sound and fury on the national stage, on campuses, and in the associations, gender equity has made only slow progress in athletics. When the U.S. Department of Education, responding to critics of Title IX, instituted a commission to review Title IX's athletics regulations in 2002, the NCAA, an early opponent of Title IX, staunchly defended the existing regulations. When the panel supported rolling back regulatory requirements, the reaction of national feminist organizations, academic associations, and a clearly articulated minority report by two members of the panel (de Varona and Foudy, 2003) led the secretary of education to accept only those panel recommendations that had full consensus. His decision allowed existing OCR interpretations and case law to stand. The effect has been increased participation and scholarships for women student-athletes. This success has come at a cost of adhering to a more expensive preexisting male model of sport, with women increasingly underrepresented in administration and coaching of women's sports and virtually absent from the coaching and administration of men's sports.

The goal of equity in athletics in both numbers and philosophy is still far from achieved. Yet the perceptions fueling resistance to Title IX persist. In a sense, a focus on Title IX's effects has diverted attention from the escalating costs of football as the primary threat to men's Olympic sports. As advocates for men's sports blame efforts to achieve gender equity for causing budget constraints, they step around the deepest questions related to the role of commercialized sports versus sports for participation on college and university campuses. The focus on gender equity as a threat also serves to discourage the building of coalitions among advocates for men's Olympic sports and women's sports; together, they might challenge the high costs of men's football, basketball, and hockey. We are left with a mystery in understanding the depth of resistance to women's participation in athletics. That mystery can only be addressed by going beyond the legal realm to the broader meaning and symbolism associated with gender norms related to sport in society and on campus. Without such a deeper understanding, campus leaders responding solely to the letter of the law may address only a portion of the issues that produce gender inequities, leading to unintended and unwanted consequences.

Summary and Implications

The vignette opening this chapter regarding disability accommodation for a prospective student-athlete illustrates the effects of this complex legal environment on campus decision-making processes related to athletics. We can imagine, for example, the initial negotiation among several sets of externally imposed NCAA and disability accommodation rules occurring through a central authority for the college or university, represented by the president's office. Over time, implementation and subsequent negotiation occur through a variety of different, and less central, channels. These channels represent a number of specialized offices and functions that interface with numerous agencies, consumers, and vendors.

For example, imagine that a previous president formally committed the university to equal opportunity, and the associated policies and procedures became institutionalized. Related institutional responsibilities evolve over time beyond the daily oversight of the president's office. That evolution produced the contemporary office of student disability services in academic affairs, which deals with day-to-day implementation of the ADA in relation to students. The disability services office employs an expert to work with students. The office connects with professional associations, legal counsel, and federal agencies informing program development to ensure compliance with interpretations of the ADA evolving through federal regulations and case law. In the absence of a major problem, the president's office may provide little further attention to daily ADA compliance. The function of disability services is institutionalized and shaped by that office and the external stakeholders with which it interacts. Professionals in disability services, through myriad relatively minor decisions and interpretations, shape campus response to the ADA far more than does the president's office.

At the same time, the institution has another avenue with ADA compliance implications opening from the athletics department to the NCAA, focusing exclusively on compliance with NCAA rules. Again, the president's office authorized the formal relationship with the NCAA and the commitment to compliance with NCAA rules. However, athletics professionals in the compliance office handle the daily negotiations and interpretations through a very different avenue from the one disability services uses. The athletics compliance staff members use the NCAA rule and find the student ineligible to compete, whereas disability services might advocate strongly for the student who is looking at the law's implications. As the NCAA rules and their interpretations evolve and change, they are communicated, and commitments are made, directly through athletics, and rarely through the president's office or the office of disability services.

The interpretation of institutional priorities, responsibilities, and means of compliance in the opening vignette differ depending on what windows to the institution the individual actors use to view them. Thus disability services and the athletics department, acting consistently with their best professional judgments, could expect the university to take very different actions relative to allowing the student to play football. A third perspective, that of legal counsel, might well yield yet different advice looking to the balancing of federal law with NCAA rules. All three see a different reality and possible solutions based on their differing professional training and responsibilities.

This chapter illustrates the disparate ways in which external laws and regulations influence athletics-related decision making and leadership at the campus level. Laws and regulations, however, are embedded in a social and cultural context in their enactment, implementation, and interpretation. The law itself does not explain, for example, the deep resistance to women's participation in athletics or the ability of institutions to enroll African American student-athletes in numbers higher than their representation in the student body at large. Those mysteries can be addressed only by going beyond the legal realm to the broader meaning and symbolism associated with gender norms related to sport in society and on campus. Without such a deeper understanding, campus leaders responding solely to the letter of the law may address only a portion of the issues producing gender or racial inequities, leading to unintended and unwanted consequences. The next chapter leads us to an analysis of the social and cultural context influencing intercollegiate athletics.

The Social and Cultural Context

EVEN AS STATE UNIVERSITY celebrated the fortunes of a national championship men's ice hockey team, it denied interested women students who played hockey the chance to compete at the varsity level. A women's club team had to climb barriers to get on the ice. The men's state-of-the-art arena with oak lockers, full weight room, the best available equipment, trainers, offices for staff and coaches, team lounge, and substantial recruiting budget contrasted with the women's pay-as-you-go effort. The women's club team paid out of pocket for ice time, often at 5 or 6 A.M., and for what equipment they did not inherit from the men's team. Despite the deep disparity in participation opportunities for men and women, placing State U. on the dark side of Title IX, repeated requests from the women's ice hockey club for varsity status went unheard. Athletics and university administrators said the budget would not allow another varsity team. These generally well-meaning and intelligent men had demonstrated commitment to opportunities for women in the university at large. Although the potential direct and indirect costs in the university's ongoing and conscious violation of Title IX could far outweigh State U.'s savings in deferring a women's varsity ice hockey team, leaders did not see a risk.

Over the next several administrations, the university gradually created a varsity women's ice hockey team. The depth and persistence of the resistance to its birth over the years can be understood through a sociocultural lens illustrating the implicit identification of intercollegiate athletics and masculinity. The decision-making process illustrates the more subtle resistance to women's substantive engagement in athletics—even among goodwilled men with a clear legal mandate. The concept of masculinity and athletics is essential to understanding the broader realm of social and cultural influences affecting collegiate leadership and decision making involving race, sexual orientation, academic culture and values, religion, and the broader cultural obsession with sports (Connell, 1995; Messner and Sabo, 1994).

Presidents, faculty, students, alumni, athletics-related administrators, coaches, and student-athletes view their sports-related experience in the college or university through lenses shaped by social and cultural norms, values, practices, and experiences. The legal and structural processes described in the preceding chapters do not explain the depth of resistance to women's full participation in intercollegiate sports. Norms are influential not only at the institutional level but also as a part of broader U.S. society. Intercollegiate athletics represent an intersection of cultures and perceptions from within and without the college or university. The different cultural contexts from which individuals and groups view sports affect the meaning they ascribe to athletics participation, sports' role in the institution, appropriate levels of financial support, and the mission of the college or university itself.

This chapter explores the influence of social and cultural beliefs about gender, race, sexual orientation, collegiate culture and academics, and sports as an institution in U.S. society on decisions made around college sports. The chapter assumes that cultural beliefs related to sports and higher education can both enhance and constrain university decision making affecting intercollegiate athletics and their governance.

Gender, Power, Privilege, and Intercollegiate Sports

Recent scholarship recognizes the importance of economic and social institutions in the construction of gender in general and masculinity in particular (Connell, 1995; Messner and Sabo, 1990). This scholarship views sport as a hierarchical and competitively structured institution central to the often invisible processes that reinforce traditional gender-role socialization.

In the realm of sport and specifically intercollegiate athletics, gender has meaning and expectations that are shaped by both contemporary and historical social contexts. Those meanings are revealed through discourses in a variety of "texts" or arenas for expression, including documents, reports, the media, policy statements, public utterances, and literature. The term *gender* specifically addresses the social and cultural expectations associated with manhood or womanhood. For example, field hockey in the United States is considered a gendered activity, associated with women and girls. In many other countries, however, field hockey is a male activity. The appropriateness of field hockey as an activity is determined not by biology but by norms that our culture ascribes to each sex. Most cultures dating from the earliest Olympiad have defined athletics as male-appropriate activity associated with virility and masculinity. Thus, Title IX's mandate for equal opportunity based in sex challenges not only the equitable distribution of resources but also a long-standing gender order.

The Gendering of Intercollegiate Athletics

The demands of Title IX present an obvious challenge to male power and dominance in intercollegiate athletics. Yet that challenge and the reaction to it are deeply embedded in the earliest history of U.S. intercollegiate athletics. Historians and sociologists of sport describe a complex set of gender dynamics in the nineteenth and twentieth centuries shaping the evolution of men's and women's athletics (Chu, 1989; Connell, 1995; Festle, 1996; Guttman, 1988, 1991; Hult, 1999; Cahn, 1994; Kane, 2001; Lucas and Smith, 1978; Messner and Sabo, 1994; Messner, 2002; Sack and Staurowsky, 1998).

Men's intercollegiate sports burst on U.S. higher education simultaneously with the emergence of the U.S. research university. They emerged from the post–Civil War era into the twentieth century when the suffrage movement challenged male dominance in U.S. society (Kidd, 1990), when Victorian expectations of masculinity conflicted with a perception that an intellectual life was more feminine in nature, and when the presidents of the new universities (or old ones in new incarnations) needed students and funds. Thus men's college sports filled several college and university needs during this period of growth: sports provided visible displays of masculinity, symbolizing the relationship between masculinity and academic institutions (Lucas and Smith, 1978; Sack and Staurowsky, 1998). They also provided a powerful tool for linking a public often wary of intellectual endeavor with a magnetic attraction, especially to college football (Toma, 2003). Harvard, Yale, Princeton, the University of Michigan, the University of Chicago, and Notre Dame are all examples of institutions in which the growth of academic reputations was similarly linked with visibility and success on the gridiron (Toma, 2003; Hardy and Berryman, 1982; Bachin, 2001).

The post–Civil War era also fostered the Protestant evangelical movement and its offspring, the concept of muscular Christianity, in which English headmasters and U.S. college presidents alike viewed competitive sports as a means to a Christian manliness (Putney, 2001; Whitson, 1990; Bachin, 2001). A reaction to the domesticity characteristic of the Victorian era, muscular Christianity further institutionalized sports as a male domain (Putney, 2001).

Women's sports were also rooted in the post–Civil War era but with the convergence of different, though related, events. The Victorian era surrounding the birth of modern football encouraged societal skepticism about the suitability of women, known then as the weaker sex, for academic work. Thus while the University of Chicago used football as a symbol of the manliness of academic work, women's colleges such as Smith College quickly incorporated physical education into their curricula to demonstrate and nurture women's strength, or at least its appearance (Wushanley, 2004; Sack and Staurowsky, 1998). Even as they challenged the norm in which women were expected to be inactive, faculty members responsible for the women's programs and the intercollegiate contests that grew from them sought programs consistent with the gender values of the times. This meant being properly feminine and, most importantly, not repeating the perceived excesses already visible in men's programs: competitive values and associated violence, commercialism, the exploitation of student-athletes, and compromises to academic values (Hardy and Berryman, 1982; Cahn, 1994). Thus separate and different women's programs did not challenge the male dominance expressed through athletics. Indeed, far more women assumed support roles as cheerleaders and spectators for men's contests than assumed roles as participants on women's teams. With some variations, women's sports were directed by women faculty members, educationally oriented, and without scholarships until the enactment of Title IX in 1972 (Acosta and Carpenter, 1985).

In the decades following the enactment of Title IX, women's administration of women's sports programs dropped from 90 percent in 1972 to 17.9 percent in 2002 (Acosta and Carpenter, 2004). The smallest percentage of women athletics directors is in NCAA Division I, which is most characterized by the image of big-time men's sports. Women's positions as head coaches of women's teams dropped from 90 percent in 1972 to 44.1 percent in 2004. Women represent under 2 percent of head coaches of men's teams (Carpenter and Acosta, 2004). Scholars cite the underrepresentation of women in coaching and leadership positions as indicative of the strong connections between sport, gender, and homophobia (Griffin, 1998; Kane, 2001; Staurowsky, 1990). Staurowsky (p. 163) writes, "There is an underlying assumption that links sports expertise with masculinity and leadership with male superiority. This assumption has permitted the notion that coaching male athletes is the exclusive responsibility of male coaches."

One might explain this pattern of men's domination of the leadership roles in sport in a number of ways. Economically, we might expect more male applicants to be attracted by the higher salaries produced in response to equal opportunity laws for coaching women's teams. However, that explanation would also predict similar applications on the part of women for coaching positions in men's sports. We could imagine that the pattern resulted from an influx into women's sports of more qualified male coaches. Although sometimes true, this explanation belies both the legions of women formally trained in coaching in physical education programs and research; for example, Anderson and Gill's study (1983) of Iowa high school basketball coaches found women more qualified than men. Those viewing men's athletics as perpetuating male dominance of societal institutions see the pattern as a response to female assertion and male power (Messner and Sabo, 1990; Messner, 2002; Sage, 1990; Oglesby, 2001).

The irony of Title IX is that its enactment in 1972 was one response to the wave of feminist activism erupting from the civil rights movements of the 1960s and that it resulted in the subordination of women's sports to the dominant male model. Further, at the very time that women's sports were falling to male governance, women collegiate physical educators were, for the most part, isolated from the support of academic feminists because of the perceived institutional sexism associated with intercollegiate sports (Creedon, 1994; Messner and Sabo, 1990). Many academic feminists viewed athletics as an instrument of male dominance in society and ignored the endeavor until more recent decades. Those professionals associated with men's sports treated women's programs with benign neglect at best. Thus women collegiate sports professionals were marginalized and isolated from inclusion as colleagues and in leadership of the sports enterprise to which they now belonged, even as the number of women student-athletes increased.

Title IX has spurred far higher participation of women in intercollegiate sports than its critics would have predicted, with 8,402 women's varsity teams in NCAA institutions in 2004, or an average of 8.32 teams per institution versus an average of 2.5 per institution in 1970 (Carpenter and Acosta, 2004). Within the NCAA and in separate professional organizations such as the National Association of Collegiate Directors of Athletics (NACDA), the National Association of Collegiate Women Athletic Administrators, the Women's Basketball Coaches Association, and various other coaches' associations, women athletics leaders continue to advocate for the ideal of a more student-centered, educational model for women's sports and women's sports leadership. Women's collegiate sports and their leadership are also supported by advocacy groups such as the National Association for Girls and Women in Sports and the Women's Sports Foundation. Despite the greater collaboration in advocacy by women's groups, the integration of women's sports into governance organizations such as the NCAA and the NAIA has nevertheless come at a cost. The structure and culture is dominated by a competitive and increasingly commercialized perspective shaped by male dominance of the athletics enterprise.

Some scholars credit the culture of masculinity in athletics for reinforcing or producing a culture that can support behaviors unacceptable to the campus at large. Although the exception, high-profile scandals around drinking, sexual favors and assault, and violence can become the focal point of institutional decision making to the detriment of attention to core institutional functions.

Homophobia and Masculinity

The cultural influence of gender reaches deeper into intercollegiate athletics than do the numbers of female and male athletes, coaches and administrators. The climate produced through the gendering of athletics can be detrimental to both athletics and the institution at large through the effects of both sexism and homophobia. Aggressive masculinity uses heterosexism and homophobia as mechanisms to enforce gender roles and male supremacy within them (Cahn, 1994; Connell, 1995; Griffin, 1998; Pharr, 1988). Griffin (p. 20) defines five ways in which sport for men ensures a gender order supporting the maintenance of presumed male superiority and female subordination: "(1) defining and reinforcing traditional conceptions of masculinity, (2) providing an acceptable and safe context for male bonding and intimacy, (3) reinforcing male privilege and female subordination, (4) establishing status among other males, and (5) reinforcing heterosexuality."

Thus even as the NCAA includes sexual orientation in its nondiscrimination policy, sport remains an arena in which differences in sexual orientation and gender identity remain taboo (Wolf-Wendel, Toma, and Morphew, 2001; Messner and Sabo, 1994; Griffin, 1998).

The heterosexual male norms of sports keep gay male athletes, coaches, and administrators closeted, reinforcing the gender order associated with athletics. The norms and practices supporting that gender order serve to keep lesbians in the closet; labeling assertive women athletes or athletics professionals as lesbian can threaten and sabotage careers (Blum, 1994; Cahn, 1994; Griffin, 1998). The power of such labeling is maintained by persistent prejudice in sport culture.

The intersection of athletics and aggressive masculinity contributes to the range of excesses—including commercialism, sexual misconduct, escalating salaries and other costs, and weak academic performance—in intercollegiate athletics subject to ongoing reform efforts. This junction can also promote values that, at their extreme, may be dysfunctional for men most bound by them: disrespect for women, disrespect for intellectual success, and reliance on physicality and violence to solve differences (Connell, 1995;

Sabo, 1994). Affirmative reasons for campus leadership to challenge both homophobia and gender hierarchies in athletics include the potential for creating a gradual shift in the underlying value structure supporting the athletics arms race including competitiveness, dominance, and power. Participation in athletics has been used to demonstrate male competitiveness, dominance, and physicality. In that setting, women athletes and coaches step out of the realm of traditional femininity, with resulting pressures to compensate in order to avoid the lesbian label. Paradoxically, sports has also been a realm central to lesbian culture, especially at times when it was socially and physically unsafe for lesbians to be out of the closet (Zipter, 1988).

The culture of sport relative to sexual orientation is increasingly at odds with campus cultures, values, and policies affirming the importance of full inclusion of all students in the college or university campus and recognition for merit rather than personal attributes. Although academic cultures increasingly view sexual orientation as irrelevant to judging a person, it remains a source of dilemmas and paradoxes within intercollegiate athletics. Both Penn State and Rice universities have had occasions in which athletics personnel used their positions to express their aversion to openly gay or lesbian participation in their programs (Lederman, 1991; Jacobson, 2002). The result was campus and national outcry calling for institutional responses supportive of nondiscrimination. No institution welcomes embarrassing national media attention to homophobic behaviors within an athletics program; such behavior is no longer acceptable in many quarters.

Homophobia in athletics has several implications for leadership. In an increasingly open societal climate, more coaches and student-athletes are willing to confront rather than accept homophobia. Consequently, campus leadership in athletics is challenged to be proactive in educational efforts or respond effectively to friction resulting from unaddressed homophobia. Ideally, progressive and clearly inclusive policies with supportive education can help reduce homophobia in an athletics program. Campus leadership, in turn, is challenged to provide the leadership fostering a cultural shift in the athletics department.

Race and Intercollegiate Athletics: Opportunity or Exploitation?

Alongside dominant social expectations around gender and sexual orientation, college sports have also been a crucible for cultural expectations and conflict regarding race. Now disproportionately represented in both football and men's and women's basketball programs (NCAA, 2004d), African American student-athletes often provide the primary basis for diversity among student bodies in many predominantly white U.S. universities. At the same time, those students graduate at lower rates than do their white teammates, enter with lower average high school grade point averages, and respond constantly to the novelty of their race on campuses lacking support for students of color (Lapchick, 1996; Edwards, 1984).

A comprehensive study of the experiences of African American student-athletes, commissioned by the NCAA Council of Presidents and conducted by the American Institutes for Research (AIR, 1989), found that the representation of African American students in sports programs is, on average, far higher than within campuses at large. The study listed the median enrollment of African Americans at NCAA Division I institutions as 4 percent, while 37 percent of Division I football players, 56 percent of men's basketball players, and 33 percent of women's basketball players were African American. In all other sports, 8 percent of student-athletes were black. A review of more contemporary but not as finely detailed NCAA data (NCAA, 2003b, 2004a) suggests these numbers remain fairly representative. The data illuminate a number of campus dilemmas.

Black student-athletes are often on predominantly white campuses where they "feel racially isolated . . . are overrepresented in football and basketball, have unreasonably high expectations of pro careers, and are uninvolved in other extracurricular activities" (Lapchick, 1996, p. 7, citing AIR, 1989). Black student-athletes find few faculty, staff, or athletics staff and administrators who are not white (Lapchick, 1996; AIR, 1989; NCAA, 2003b). The time demands of the sport, the greater number of visible black role models in professional sports than in other roles, and the ability of the coach to withdraw a scholarship assures that student-athletes will make their sport a primary focus of their college experience. The specter of exploitation lies in the ability of most institutions to recruit black student-athletes and the inability to recruit comparable numbers of blacks who are not on sports scholarships. With few campus advocates to speak on their behalf and faced with a risk of losing scholarships, African American student-athletes are limited in their ability to question institutional dynamics related to race.

White coaches are often perceived as discriminating in subtle or overt ways, for example, in segregation of black players by position, differential recruitment practices, and differential advising (Wiggins, 1991; AIR, 1989; Lapchick, 1996). Lapchick (1996, p. 9) notes that such responses may reflect actual discrimination or mistrust of white coaches, observing, "To say that most or even many White coaches are racist is a great exaggeration. But most White coaches were raised with White values in a White culture. The norm for them is what is important for a White society." Johnson (2001) and McIntosh (1990) describe the subtle ways in which those with social privilege are unaware of their unearned privilege and its effects on those without. In the case of college sports, white coaches, faculty, and administrators may be blind to their own privilege and unable to see and understand the experience of the black student-athletes they lead.

Stereotypes of black athletes affect both their athletic and academic experiences. White stereotypes of African Americans result in lower academic expectations, with staff channeling those students toward majors that continue eligibility but do not necessarily ensure career success and, at the extreme, making negative comments about the capabilities of African American student-athletes. Even the possibility of stereotyping implicit in a predominantly white environment can adversely affect black academic performance through the phenomenon that Steele (1997) described as stereotype threat. Stereotypic attitudes toward student-athletes may blind majority coaches, administrators, faculty, and students to the possibility that the imbalance between African American student-athletes and students in the general student population is a result of policies assuring exclusion in realms not depending on stereotypical physical prowess.

At the same time, unrealistic stereotypes in many black communities about the opportunities available in professional sports can serve to undermine the importance of the education that an athletics scholarship can make possible (Edwards, 1984). The lingering limitations in opportunities in other sectors of the economy often leaves sports as one of the few visible sources of black role models, especially for the black male. Messner (1990) noted in a study of high school boys that white middle- and upper middle-class boys shifted their aspirations from athletics as wider choices for long-term educational and professional possibilities became apparent. Minority men, on the other hand, viewed sports as a source of respect in a system of constrained opportunities in which wider educational and professional choices were not apparent.

The stereotyping of black student-athletes is often fueled by recruiting and admissions practices that follow significantly lower high school grades and test scores among black student-athletes in comparison to nonblack student-athletes (Shulman and Bowen, 2001; AIR, 1989; Sage, 1990). However, black student-athletes graduate, on average, in higher numbers than do black students who are not athletes (NCAA, 2004d). This offers evidence that both participation in athletics and academic support programs to help assure academic success have an impact. Admission considerations for black student-athletes, in the absence of a full institutional commitment to a multicultural environment, raise the question of whether institutions seek to exploit the student-athlete or offer him or her a substantive opportunity. At a national level, efforts to raise academic standards for participation in college sports inevitably disproportionately affect black student-athletes given practices allowing lower grades and test scores. Against this backdrop, it is not surprising that the apparent limiting of opportunity, either for education or athletics notoriety, reinforces perceptions of exploitation.

The relative absence of blacks in coaching and administrative roles to serve as role models, provide counsel, and signal professional opportunity symbolizes different institutional values depending on the viewer. For black student-athletes, the absence represents hypocrisy on the part of institutions that regularly produce action plans to increase their diversity (Shropshire, 1996). For nonblacks, it symbolizes, if at an unconscious level, an affirmation of the status quo.

Although coaches and athletics administrators make most of the decisions affecting the dynamics of race in athletics, effective leadership at the campus level recognizes both the campuswide opportunities and responsibilities inherent in those decisions. Campus leaders can set expectations for the racial climate in both the athletics department and the campus at large. Failure to do so assures both a compromised academic and athletic experience for black student-athletes and fuels racial disharmony within the campus.

Sports and Academic Culture

Black student-athletes and white teammates participate in a growing academic-athletic cultural divide. Tensions between academic and athletic goals and values have characterized the uniquely U.S. marriage between sports and academics almost since its inception in the nineteenth century (Bailey and Littleton, 1991; Bowen and Levin, 2003; Guttman, 1982; Lucas and Smith, 1978; Shulman and Bowen, 2001; Sperber, 1990; Smith, 1988; and Thelin and Wiseman, 1989). Thelin (1996) describes the series of reform efforts, including the founding of the NCAA, intended to bring the athletics enterprise more in tune with the academic values of the institutions housing them, especially in those programs characterized as big-time sports. The efforts were typically initiated through studies often sponsored by national commissions external to the sports establishment; examples are the Savage report (Savage and others, 1929), sponsored by the Carnegie Commission on Teaching, and George Hanford's 1974 report sponsored by the American Council on Education. Recent commissions and reports have lent particular attention to the academic side of the athletics-versus-academics equation.

Since 1990, the Knight Foundation has sponsored a major commission on intercollegiate athletics that produced two major reports a decade apart (Knight Foundation Commission on Intercollegiate Athletics [Knight Commission], 1991, 2001) and recent hearings on the financing of college sports. NCAA studies provide ample evidence that the graduation rates of student-athletes in men's Division I-A revenue sports have been considerably lower than those of the student population at large. Such studies, and recommendations by the Knight Commission, have prompted NCAA legislation on initial eligibility standards and NCAA and institutional efforts to improve the academic experience of the student-athlete, including academic support services and awards for academic achievement.

Recent studies suggest that there is a growing academic-athletic divide even at smaller and more academically selective institutions that do not provide scholarships. The Mellon Foundation has sponsored some of the most substantive research on athletics and academics, producing two major studies, *The Game of Life: College Sports and Educational Values* (Shulman and Bowen, 2001) and *Reclaiming the Game: College Sports and Educational Values* (Bowen and Levin, 2003). In addition, the NCAA's research department annually produces a full array of reports analyzing aspects of the athletics experience and the programs supporting it exemplified by the *NCAA Student Athlete Ethnicity Report* (NCAA, 2004d).

Bowen and Levin (2003) conducted an important study of the effects of participating in athletics on student-athletes and the colleges and universities they attend. They premised their study on the notion "that there is an urgent need to recognize that the traditional values of college sports are threatened by the emergence of a growing 'divide' between intercollegiate athletics and the academic missions of many institutions that are free of the special problems of 'big-time sports'" (p. 2).

Their work was prompted by a prior study (Shulman and Bowen, 2001), which found a widening gap between academics and athletics at a group of highly selective institutions that avoided the trappings of the big time, at least partially, by offering no athletics scholarships, competing only at levels below Division I-A, and expressing commitments to the amateur ideal. Bowen and his coauthors (Bowen and Levin, 2003) sought to understand results from the first study, suggesting that college athletes underperformed academically in comparison to similarly prepared nonathletic classmates.

The two studies found that the culture of smaller colleges, generally assumed to be free from the abuses of big-time sports, was more affected by the selective admission of athletes than was the culture of large universities. This might result from a higher proportion of the student body consisting of recruited student-athletes. Further, Bowen and Levin (2003) found that student-athletes who were recruited by coaches were more prone to underperformance academically than were student-athletes who were accepted and then sought to participate in athletics as "walk-ons." The study, which included historic comparisons, found that the gap was steadily widening over time rather than narrowing as the commercialism and national attention to sports continues to grow.

Sports and the American Psyche

The media have been instrumental in the escalated commercialization and centrality of sport to U.S. life. As television brought sports into our living rooms from the 1950s to the present, the advertising dollars, television rights, equipment, and jobs associated with all the elements of the enterprise increasingly made sports big business. With the homogeneous control of the media, the values reflected in the sports juggernaut continued to reflect those of white, heterosexual, aggressive masculinity (Creedon, 1994; Creedon, Cramer, and Granitz, 1994; Messner and Sabo, 1994; Sage, 1990). Local newspapers and television news teams typically have a larger staff of sports writers than, for example, education writers. When the media represent sports, they often reinforce stereotypic images and values related to men, women, and people of color (Cahn, 1994; Creedon, 1994).

At the same time, the media can also reflect changing social values. The U.S. public now sees strong and competitive women basketball players in the televised NCAA national tournament and a women's professional league affiliated with the male National Basketball Association. Indeed, the women's NCAA basketball championship game had a larger television audience in 2004 than did the men's championship. The continued pattern of male efforts to control women's sports, however, is demonstrated in the scheduling of women's professional competition only in the summer, when it will not conflict with the National Basketball Association men's teams, which sponsor the women's league.

Sport plays a significant role in U.S. culture and its economy. Super Bowl Sunday has become an undeclared national holiday. Families spend recreational time engaged with increasing numbers of organized sports from young children to adults. Gerdy's description (2002, p. 255) of contemporary sport describes an arena more about commerce and entertainment than personal growth and education: "Sport is corporate skyboxes, sneaker deals, television contracts, free agency, salary caps, coaching 'packages,' academic fraud, trading and signing shows, sports memorabilia, traveling 'all-star' teams of seven-year-olds, win, win, win, sell more product—hats, jackets, commemorative coffee cups, all-star, all-world, all-university. It all adds up to an American addiction."

Against this background, colleges and universities understandably look to high-profile sports to generate brand recognition for their institutions in the competition for student enrollments. The chapter "Economics and the Athletics System" discusses this strategy and its effectiveness in more detail.

Conclusion: Social and Cultural Shaping of Decision Making in Intercollegiate Athletics

College sports are a key connector between the college or university and differing class communities and communities of color. College sports are also a crucible reflecting evolving cultural expectations related to masculinity and femininity. The decision-making hierarchies in both athletics and colleges and universities at large continue to be homogeneous in gender, race, class, and sexual orientation. The resulting homogeneity of experience and culture may leave decision makers blind to important educational, ethical, and legal dynamics related to communities of difference.

In the absence of systematic and intentional interrogation of small and large athletics-related decisions by decision makers, leaders can continue to support the status quo. This all too often involves the unintentional exploitation of African American student-athletes, denies comparable opportunities and support to women student-athletes, and binds male student-athletes to often unwanted expectations of aggressive masculinity that serve neither academic nor social development. Resistance to male dominance in sport can be difficult at best due to peer pressure and broader societal influences conveyed through social and political institutions including the family, the media, and the schools. The economic context also reinforces the social and cultural dynamics of college sports, as the next chapter will discuss.

Economics and the Athletics System

FOOTBALL DOESN'T TOP the list of cultural priorities in a state where the first snow flurries often occur in October and public schools in the northern third of the state still close for the potato harvest three weeks each fall. Basketball, though, gets folks through the long, cold, winters in isolated rural towns where businesses often close for February school break to follow the fortunes of the high school basketball team in the state tournament. At the state university, football rarely filled the seats in the stadium, which was smaller and shabbier than the larger high school stadiums. Deferred maintenance due to budget cuts over the years allowed the old wooden stadium to deteriorate. The fire marshal finally condemned the structure as unsafe.

Rallied by a former football coach for whom the current coach had played quarterback, a group of local business people raised funds for a new ten thousand–seat stadium promoted as the best in the region. A local philanthropist donated a three million–dollar matching grant for the new stadium, which was in use by fall. It provided an artificial turf for field hockey and recreational uses as well as for football. Recognizing the investment that the community had made in football, the university committed to support the team for competitiveness, restoring football scholarships that had been cut to reallocate for budget support across the athletics program. A maintenance fund was established, and the university made a long-term commitment to continue the current coach with an immediate raise and an eventual salary level among the highest in the institution. Within several years, the team was competing for a national Division II-A championship. The stadium nevertheless was rarely full. Faculty and students continued to protest ever higher resources dedicated to sports, especially football.

This fictionalized account illustrates a variety of ways in which the economics of college sports affect college and university decision making, culture, and athletics leadership. From one perspective, a group of community supporters stepped up to support the university in its time of need, with appropriate safeguards to protect the investment. From another perspective, an unrepresentative set of commercial interests opportunistically used the university's moment of need to leverage its commitment to a sport threatened with extinction, encumbering future university funds in doing so. Although each view interprets the events differently, all the views share the assumption that an infusion of money influenced the related decision making. Further, each view assumes a level of intention and analysis on the part of the actors that may be unreasonable in the face of the limited time, information, and resources available to the decision makers.

Consider the complex challenge the president faced with limited time for response. On the one hand, there were commitments to several years of football scholarships, game schedules, and nonsporting events such as commencement in the only facility on campus that could hold several thousand people. The challenge was compounded by substandard field hockey facilities that could cause injury to players even while Title IX demanded upgrading. Finally, football was considered central to membership in a peer set of institutions in which football and its trappings are central to public identity as a "real university." On the other hand, the president is also presented with a gift horse by respected community members with long-term institutional roots and political and economic clout within the institution and the state. The president faced these challenges and opportunities with time constraints imposed by harsh winters that require sufficient progress on new construction to allow protection from the elements for work over the winter. In addition, the press of many competing decisions in areas considered more central to the university's teaching, learning, and research missions demanded time and attention. In short, decisions like the choice to accept gift money to build a new stadium are often made under duress.

Leaders who make decisions under fire rarely have the luxury of analyzing preferences underlying values, searching for all possible alternatives, or gathering information to assess the relative merits of each. Instead, institutional decision makers, beset with the unrelenting pace of competing demands on their time and attention, are forced to defer to the advice of staff who, in turn, use incomplete information to arrive at immediate solutions. Further, the multiple goals and expectations for an athletics program, each with its own set of advocates and constituents, compete for resources with the academic and other programs constituting a university. Access to external resources addresses one key impediment to favorable decisions in arenas characterized by scarce resources. However, such decisions rarely come without strings attached and without affecting future commitments and priorities. Thus a decision about reconstruction of a condemned facility becomes a long-term commitment to a long-contested, highly resource-dependent sport without thorough consideration of collegial governance.

Commercialization of Intercollegiate Athletics and the Entrepreneurial University

Athletics was among the first programs to bring entrepreneurial strategies to colleges and universities that were traditionally described as ivory towers for their independence and isolation from the external environment (Bok, 2003). Indeed, Walter Byers, the first executive director of the NCAA, was charged on his appointment in 1951 with two missions, "Keeping college sports clean while generating millions of dollars each year as income for the colleges" (Byers with Hammer, 1995, p. 5). Discussing the explosive growth in college sports in the period until his retirement in 1987, Byers observed that, "as the rewards for winning multiplied, so did breaking the rules and cheating" (p. 5). Colleges and universities have become increasingly entrepreneurial in the past decades in response to decreasing resources and increasing demands (Bok, 2003; Clark, 1998; Kezar, 2004). Decisions related to research facilities and related curricular priorities may also be influenced by the flow of external dollars. Thus consideration of the commercialization of athletics needs to take into account a broader context of incentives and affirmation for entrepreneurship across university communities.

Prior chapters have already addressed important elements related to the economics of intercollegiate athletics: institutional and external organizational structures and the evolution of commercialized football; the impact of legal mandates including antitrust law, tax law, and federal nondiscrimination laws on resource flows; the ongoing tensions between academic and athletics values affecting internal spending priorities; and the role of institutional and societal values involving gender, race, masculinity, academic values, and cultural values regarding sports.

This chapter will briefly identify the key themes related to the economics of college sports and some of the myths they reveal. More centrally, it addresses economic issues through an analysis that considers college sports in the context of external demands and unintended outcomes.

Economic Themes and Myths

The central themes that recur across the literature related to the economics of intercollegiate athletics include the following:

The challenges of an athletics arms race escalating the resources required to maintain a sports program perceived as competitive among its peers
The increased commercialization of athletics
The costs and markets associated with the labor pool of student-athletes and coaches doing the work of college sports
The perceived impact of Title IX on the financing of college sports
The perceived secondary benefits from college sports in revenues through increased enrollments and increased giving

There are other significant economic themes and other ways of categorizing than those selected here. Our hope is that this somewhat overlapping list will provide a substantial overview and a basis from which to consider areas not represented.

The Athletics Arms Race

Although the arms-race label reflects late twentieth-century Cold War experience, the phenomenon it describes in intercollegiate athletics predates the First World War. Simply put, it represents the efforts of athletics programs and the institutions they represent to assure the resources, facilities, and student-athletes to play on a level field with peer institutions. However, the field is never perceived as level. Like the real arms race, the athletics arms race reflects the desire of coaches, student-athletes, and sometimes institutions to gain a competitive advantage. Newer and better competition venues, more coaches, luxury locker rooms with weight rooms and lounges to attract the best recruits, higher salaries to attract the best coaches, and luxury skyboxes to attract corporate support are all elements of the drive to be bigger and better.

The athletics arms race has profound effects on the cost of athletics programs, with nearly threefold increases in total average expenses between 1985 and 2001 across each NCAA division above Division III. For example, the average expenditures for the universities in Division I-A were $6.9 million in 1985 and $23.2 million in 2001 (Fulks, 2002a). Perhaps more relevant to the arms race is the largest individual Division I-A institutional expenditure budget in 2001 of $52.1 million, a figure more than twice the Division I-A average of $23.2 million. Greater still were the largest single institutional revenues at $79.6 million, an exceptional figure doubtless fueling the aspirations of peer institutions (Fulks, 2002a).

Contrary to popular mythology, on average, both large and small colleges and universities lose money on intercollegiate athletics. As athletics expenditures have escalated since the 1980s, revenues have not matched their growth. As a result, the vast majority of colleges and universities must pay for growing deficits between athletics revenues, which generally include budgeted institutional funds, and growing expenses generated to meet perceived competitive pressures. As described earlier, only Division I-A institutions operated athletics programs in 2001 in which, on average, revenues exceeded expenses (Fulks, 2002a). Otherwise, the average 2001 athletics deficits described in NCAA reports range from $400,000 to $1.2 million and to $3.4 million if institutional support is not included (Fulks, 2002a). Differences of this magnitude illustrate the growing divide between the haves, represented by the most competitive of Division I-A institutions, and have-nots, represented by institutions that choose not to compete or are unable to compete at that level in college sports.

The magnitude of expenditures for athletics is important in considering the impact of college sports in the marketplace. Even though most programs operate at substantial deficits, the expenditures of athletics programs generate large numbers of economic stakeholders at the local and national level, many with political influence that comes with business success. College sports, for example, sustain substantial numbers of jobs, contracts, advertising dollars, travel agencies, caterers and restaurants, apparel and equipment manufacturers, and construction enterprises. In addition, athletics scholarships, for the most part provided by gifts, fund enrollments for hundreds of students at a given college or university in a given year—a number that has a significant impact on funding for academic programs. For more typical institutions of higher education, demand for admission does not allow highly selective admissions. In such cases, students attending on athletics scholarships represent a substantial source of tuition revenue that those universities could not easily replace if they eliminated athletics scholarships.

The arms race, especially at the big-time Division I level, and its implications are discussed at length in a number of works in addition to reports from the Knight Foundation Commission on Intercollegiate Athletics (Knight Commission, 1991, 2001; Sack and Staurowsky, 1998; Shulman and Bowen, 2001; Sperber, 1990; Thelin, 1996; Zimbalist, 1999). But the issues do not stop at the big-time programs. Bowen and Levin (2003) discuss a growing academic-athletic divide that affects elite Division III institutions in ways that effectively echo the upper divisions and result in arms-race behavior. The forces they attribute to escalating the arms race include the following: increased specialization among athletes created by the formalization and intensity of sport at youth levels; the professionalization and specialization of coaching exacerbated by recruiting pressures for those more specialized student-athletes; national championship competitions and pressure within some institutions to aspire to them; pressures on coaches to win at any cost; and some related, though unintended, interacting effects of Title IX with the male model of athletics implicit in these trends. Although Bowen and Levin studied elite institutions, little would suggest a different pattern in less selective institutions.

Imitation within and among colleges and universities, and within the NCAA, has a multiplier effect among peer institutions to keep up with presumed competition and among aspiring institutions to move up. Division I-A football and basketball generate ticket sales, media contracts, and championship guarantees worth millions and, in the case of the NCAA and CBS, billions of dollars. However, NCAA rules encourage sports that are not expected to generate revenues to emulate football and basketball in scholarships and coaching staffs. Thelin (2000) describes this pattern as an unacknowledged revolution in intercollegiate athletics, with the demand for more coaches and more scholarships occurring prior to the impact of Title IX. Across institutions, imitation or emulation occurs in the effort to be more like the more prestigious colleges or universities. Thus when a major power recruits a football coach with a million-dollar contract, the pattern reverberates across the university's organizational field. Thus professed equity drives coaching salaries up—perhaps not to a million dollars but to a lesser figure that may nevertheless exceed most faculty salaries in the same institution.

Division III institutions are not immune from the arms race. They averaged 25 percent increases in their athletics budgets in just the two years between 1999 and 2001 (Fulks, 2002b). In every division above Division III, the percentage increase was highest between 1985 and 1989, ranging from average increases of 33 percent in Division II with football to 75 percent in Division I-AAA. Division I-A increases averaged 40 percent. (Fulks, 2002a, 2002b, 2002c). These were the years in which the gender equity mandate of Title IX was suspended due to the U.S. Supreme Court decision in *Grove City College v. Bell* (1984).

Although engaging in an athletics arms race is not new for colleges and universities, the magnitude of spending is profoundly different from before the 1980s. The invention and mass consumption of television began in the 1950s; television's influence with its associated advertising dollars ballooned in more recent decades, fueling the arms race through a massive infusion of capital into intercollegiate athletics.

Escalating Commercialism

Escalating costs, generated by the athletics arms race, created the need for new revenues to pay them. Given limited institutional resources, especially in competition with academic departments, athletics departments are encouraged to engage in entrepreneurial activities. Rather than decreasing costs, athletics departments have tried to meet the costs for growing programs by reaching beyond traditional revenue sources of ticket sales, television revenues, and donations (Thelin and Wiseman, 1989). To support their efforts toward financial self-sufficiency, athletics departments within larger universities typically have their own fundraising, corporate relations, and media relations staff, separate from the department(s) handling those functions for the university as a whole. Internally, they have increasingly drawn on student fees to help subsidize athletics.

The 2001 Knight Commission report cites the growing commercialization of college sports especially in the 1990s. Higher education and its athletics programs have been the beneficiaries of massive television and footwear contracts and the sale of space in stadiums and arenas to advertisers. In addition, the naming of facilities after major donors and the sale of skyboxes and privileged parking spaces further commercialize college sports at levels that far exceed earlier eras.

The pressures toward entrepreneurialism that drive the current commercializing of college sports are fueled by the larger society. Our national obsession with sports, discussed in the previous chapter, means that college sports are a profitable vehicle for advertising goods appealing to sports fans through signs in arenas, advertising during televised games or live events, promotions, and the visible use of equipment and manufacturers' logos on uniforms and equipment. With manufacturers offering sneaker contracts even to high school student-athletes and the pressures high to keep up with the Joneses, resistance to the forces of commercialism has become increasingly difficult for individuals and universities. Further, although the long-term implications of commercialism involve the university or college's reputation, the path to full-blown commercialism is built through a series of small decisions, often by coaches, athletics staff, and administrators; once institutionalized, movement along this path becomes nearly impossible to reverse. An evolving web of formal contracts, standard operating procedures, financial stakeholders, and simple habits conspire against the success of heroic measures to stop the current pattern.

The changing social and economic context of universities has placed even greater pressures toward entrepreneurialism on today's athletics programs. That changing context extends within the university far beyond athletics. With tuitions at levels eliciting threats of government intervention and state revenues leveling or declining, colleges and universities have been faced with the need to generate new resources to support the enterprise. As a result, there is increasing pressure for university-industrial partnerships, contract research, and direct services (Bok, 2003; Kezar, 2004). As with athletics, such entrepreneurship is fueled by those in business and government, with resources and priorities often far removed from teaching and learning.

Economic studies of sport describe big-time intercollegiate athletics as a market dominated by a cartel, the NCAA. The NCAA controls prices, or wages, for student-athletes through rules related to scholarships and limitations on remuneration. The cartel also regulates the duration, intensity of usage, and subsequent mobility during college careers of the inputs (student-athletes); regulates competitions; seeks to maximize profits for its members; informs cartel members about market conditions and transactions; tries to police member behavior through a structure of rules; and penalizes members for infractions of rules (Fleisher, Goff, and Tollison, 1992; Koch, 1971; Sack, 1982; Sage, 1982; Zimbalist, 1999).

The business of intercollegiate athletics is unique in another way: No other industry "manages not to pay its principal producers a wage or a salary" (Zimbalist, 1999, p. 6). These analyses assume an intentionality and order to decision making related to intercollegiate athletics. Such an analysis belies the history, which demonstrates a combination of multiple actors, chance, cultural values, and growth of the modern university converging initially around football and later extending to other sports.

The NCAA originated around football and quickly diversified to regulate all sports. However, the protection of football and later basketball and their revenues remains central to the NCAA's focus. As the television marketplace and large stadiums allow some institutions particularly high revenues, the NCAA's cartel-like status is being challenged around the designation of particular athletics conferences for automatic access to football Bowl Championship Series (BCS) competition. As Division I universities fall within either the have or have-not categories by virtue of eligibility to participate in the BCS, the NCAA is caught in a dilemma: those privileged by the arrangement threaten to go independent of the NCAA if their favored status is threatened and the have-nots threaten antitrust action against the NCAA for excluding them from the BCS (Suggs, 2003b).

The commercialization of intercollegiate athletics raises issues related to the economics and governance of athletics within the university. The Knight Commission (1991) describes athletics programs as a parallel universe beyond the control of academia as they respond to the dynamics of the sports marketplace. Athletics serves also as a kind of canary in the mineshaft, testing the effects of commercialism across higher education. Former Harvard president Derek Bok (2003, pp. 35–36) comments on the commercialization of athletics and higher education, "In one sense, of course, they are a special case, affecting a small number of students, and a set of activities quite separate from the central mission of the education. Yet athletics are the oldest form of commercialization in American higher education. As such, they have important lessons to teach about attempts to make money from campus activity and the perils they hold for even the most eminent institutions."

The Student-Athlete: Student or Employee?

College sports at every level have grown increasingly specialized. Coaching staffs, the expected commitment of student-athletes, recruitment of student-athletes based on their athletic prowess, and in many institutions, financial aid for tuition and living expenses are all responses to this specialization. Coaching salaries have increased in major sports and major universities to levels exceeding those of university presidents, vice presidents, and even state governors. Recruiting has become a key part of a college coach's job at every level. This often conveys to student-athletes that the college or university's primary interest is in their athletic skills, regardless of their academic interests or aptitude. Big-time football and later basketball were both born in collegiate settings. These sports represented a clear shift from sport for participation value to sport for spectator-entertainment value. An academic philosophy of amateurism, in which student-athletes competed without pay as a student activity, justified including revenue-producing intercollegiate athletics in academic institutions. However, increased commercialism creates arguments for fair payment of student-athletes in revenue-producing sports (Sack, 1982; Zimbalist, 1999; Atwell, 2001). The separation between amateur values and the realities of commercialization marks a kind of line in the sand between the faculty view of the university's academic mission and a view of athletics as an end in itself.

The institution of college sports is part of two other institutions: U.S. higher education and U.S. sports. Recruited student-athletes are sensitive to the fact that college sports have become big business even in relatively small programs. Student-athletes can see a growing list of others who benefit financially at escalating levels from their labors. For many, the opportunity to continue playing a sport they love, team fellowship, and access to a college education is sufficient incentive to participate in college sports. For others, the level of expenditures and revenues associated with sports and the excesses they often reflect raise the specter of exploitation. In larger programs, millions of dollars flow through athletics departments on the basis of unpaid labor. As discussed in the chapter "The Legal and Regulatory Context," the recruitment of African American student-athletes specifically to revenue sports of basketball and football can lend a layer of perceived racism to concerns of exploitation. This perception is fueled in the absence of a comparable presence of African American students across a college or university and by African American student-athlete graduation rates lower than those of the student body at large. Much of the literature related to the economics of college sports addresses the dilemma of amateurism in the context of big business and the implications for exploitation based on amateur status, race, and social class (Sack, 1982; Sack and Staurowsky, 1998; Zimbalist, 1999).

A further complication shaping the perspective of student-athletes in football and basketball is the role of colleges and universities as a farm system for the professional leagues. This effectively requires college attendance for those aspiring to professional careers in football or basketball regardless of academic interest or aptitude. Professional baseball, which predated intercollegiate athletic competition in the sport, sponsors a system of training leagues allowing potential major league players to learn and to prove themselves in a competitive setting with pay. Participants are not required to have a college education, although potential college players would give up eligibility if they played on a professional farm team. Some of the few baseball players likely to be sufficiently skilled to play professionally choose to take a scholarship and build experience at the college level. Others go directly to professional farm teams.

Football and basketball do not provide the option of professional developmental leagues outside higher education. For historic and economic reasons, college play has become a prerequisite for drafting by professional football and basketball leagues (with certain and growing exceptions) regardless of the athlete's interest or aptitude in attaining a college education. Although the lifetime earnings associated with a college degree make it a valuable commodity for those student-athletes who acquire the degree, its requirement for professional athletes makes little sense beyond the economic benefit of providing professional leagues a pool of trained recruits without an investment of capital and human resources.

One effect of growing commercialism and the question of exploitation may be a sense of decreasing loyalty and institutional identification by student-athletes. In studying the lifetime effects of athletics participation on students, Bowen and Levin (2003) found that alumni giving among student-athletes was below that of nonathlete peers in more recent years. In the 1950s and subsequent decades, the reverse was true. The modern practice of recruiting student-athletes to a college or university for athletics skills, generating institutional benefits in identity or resources, would not appear to promote institutional loyalty. The dynamic is compounded by time demands on student-athletes, limiting their participation in the kind of broader student experience that builds institutional connections and loyalty.

Title IX Impact

Earlier discussions have addressed many of the economic myths, perceptions, and misperceptions related to Title IX. Thelin (2000) and de Varona and Foudy (2003) address in considerable detail the escalation of athletics spending independent of Title IX. Even though the economic gains of team elimination were not high, some institutions chose to cut nonrevenue men's sports to move toward Title IX compliance in participation rates. Few pursued the alternative of collective action to reduce the size of team rosters and the number of football scholarships, often numbering twice the maximum roster of a professional football team. The choices that institutions of higher education made to address Title IX by increasing rather than reducing spending on men's football and basketball is already viewed as evidence of further commitment to the elusive brass ring of new revenues. Yet the myth persists that Title IX is forcing the elimination of men's sports teams (Thelin, 2000; de Varona and Foudy, 2003).

The growing role of commercial interests in college sports and internal expectations of external fundraising often reinforces patterns of gender inequity. Driven by perceived tastes of television sports audiences, television contracts, advertising, and corporate sponsorships rarely favor women's sports over men's and particularly over basketball and football. The external flow of capital based on perceived male identification with sport reinforces internal arguments to support the programs producing the revenues. In turn, male-associated assumptions of external markets deny women's sports the public access to promote a greater audience. The larger cable television audience in March 2004 for the NCAA women's basketball championship than for the men's championship on a major broadcast network provides clear evidence that the U.S. public may show a greater interest in women's sports than advertisers and networks believe.

Secondary Benefits and Costs to Intercollegiate Athletics

A number of studies attempt to assess the relationship of athletics success and both giving to the college or university and enrollment. In a thorough review, Staurowsky (2002) notes little or weak empirical evidence showing athletics support yielding increased alumni giving for colleges and universities (citing, among others, Frey, 1985; Gerdy, 2002; Zimbalist, 1999; Sack and Staurowsky, 1998; Shulman and Bowen, 2001; Sperber, 2000; Thelin, 1994). While Rhodes and Gerking (2000), for example, found a positive effect on levels of alumni giving based on year-to-year changes in athletics success, the effect was weak compared to the role of student and faculty quality in attracting gifts.

Evidence of the relationship between athletics success and applications and enrollments is similarly ambiguous. Toma and Cross (1998) found a positive effect of championship seasons in Division I-A football on numbers of applications in the year of and years following the championship.

Toma (2003) elaborates in a later work on the role of a successful football program in creating a distinctive national brand identity for an institution that can invest at a high level in big-time football. Brand identity can, as with a number of institutions historically, provide a boost to reputation and visibility. That boost can translate to enhanced academic quality over time through positive effects on faculty hiring, giving, and student applications. There can be adverse effects to enhanced visibility as well, as evidenced by Toma's examination of the impact of athletics-based scandals on giving and enrollments (Toma, 1999).

Shulman and Bowen (2001) surveyed alumni from the 1951, 1976, and 1989 classes at thirty selective institutions with athletics programs. They are institutions Toma (2003) would identify as having strong brand identity as a function of their academic programs, name recognition, and selectivity. Shulman and Bowen found that a majority of the alumni advocated for decreased emphasis on athletics in their respective institutions while advocating increased emphasis on undergraduate teaching, residential life, intellectual freedom, other extracurricular activities, broad liberal arts education, and a diverse student body. The only other priority to which alumni gave a negative score was institutional commitment to faculty research. Coincidentally, faculty research is a second area courting external funds that can subtly shape institutional mission and identity.

Summarizing the Impact of the Economics of Intercollegiate Athletics

The economic system associated with intercollegiate athletics has often left presidents and other institutional leaders holding a tiger by the tail. College sports have become big business, tied to powerful interests, especially in resource-poor environments, and only loosely coupled to the institution's academic goals and aspirations. The athletics arms race, lucrative commercial interests, coaching salaries, increased tuition costs affecting scholarship budgets—all conspire to reward entrepreneurial activity on the part of athletics departments and the institutions housing them.

For most institutions, aspiring toward great financial rewards and enhanced academic reputation for athletics success is as reasonable as student-athletes assuming they will play in professional leagues after graduation. It happens just often enough to feed aspirations for resources and prestige, yielding for the majority more disappointment and debt than success.

The size and complexity of the external markets associated with intercollegiate athletics make the enterprise particularly difficult for administrative decision makers to control. The interests of the sports-related markets may be inconsistent with the academic market. Yet the web binding their interests is typically too complex to master without time and attention—scarce resources denied to the typical president. Instead, those with athletics expertise are likely to have the most immediate information to advise leaders about decision alternatives. Like those in any other professional realm, athletics professionals are likely to see the institution and available options through lenses shaped by their training and experience in an increasingly commercial endeavor. They rarely have either the training or experience to weigh athletics missions in the context of the college or university's academic mission. Academic administrators, on the other hand, who might share in the decision making, lack the expertise in the highly specialized and increasingly entrepreneurial world of collegiate sports.

A leadership conundrum results from this complex mix of institutional and environmental forces. Given financial stresses on the institution's academic core, faculty and academic administrators may encourage decreased dependency by athletics programs on institutional resources. External markets have been increasingly willing to respond to the financial needs of sports programs. As a result of increased financial autonomy, institutional control weakens even more over an enterprise that critics already view as out of control relative to the college or university's academic mission.

Summary, Conclusions, and Recommendations

A LOCAL BUSINESS COLLEGE serving area students effectively recreated its identity in the past decade by expanding its curriculum and adding graduate programs. The college capped the identity shift by adding a football team coached by a well-known local high school coach. Soon after, it appointed a revered retired university baseball coach to the newly created position of vice president for sports leadership. The new vice president made a major gift and raised additional funds for a state-of-the-art baseball diamond bearing his name. A minor league professional baseball team contracted to play in the facility in the summers, adding to the public flow to the campus. The institution changed its athletics affiliation from National Association for Intercollegiate Athletics to the more visible National Collegiate Athletics Association (NCAA). These sports-related initiatives generated far more local media coverage, visibility, and name recognition than had a decade of curricular innovations. The institution no longer struggles for enrollments to ensure survival as it did twenty years ago. Instead, it has built both a new public identity and growing enrollments statewide.

Has athletics been successful in creating a sense of a real university, or is the institution beginning down a path of athletics escalation to the potential detriment of its long-term budgetary health, academic mission, and academic reputation? Regardless of a conclusion that will be more shaped by perception than empirical data, the situation leaves no doubt that the belief in athletics as an institution builder is as alive today as it was with the marriage of football and the emerging universities at the turn of the twentieth century.

This vignette reveals the complex interaction of external structures, external rules, perceived societal values and culture, politics, and perceived economic benefits in shaping athletics offerings and administrative structures. Perhaps most significantly, it exemplifies the fact that concerns related to athletics cannot be simply dismissed as a Division I-A phenomenon. These can and do have a significant impact even on non-elite Division III institutions.

The Athletics System and Intersecting Environmental Forces

None of the four relatively focused lenses with which we have viewed intercollegiate athletics and campus leadership (structural, legal, social and cultural, and economic) fully captures the complexity of the enterprise. Yet each provides some unique insights and implications, as the previous chapters indicate. Together, they reveal properties and processes related to the broad impact of the external environment on campus decision making related to intercollegiate athletics.

We have described a world in which administrators make decisions, of necessity, without the luxury of time or resources for the thoughtful and thorough deliberation implied by economic or classical organizational theory. Instead, institutional, athletics, and faculty leaders confront opportunities in an ever-changing context of competing choices, participants, problems, and solutions dependent on their experience to guide them (Cohen and March, 1974). Although the issues related to intercollegiate athletics may be long-term and predictable, they are somewhat less familiar to most administrative and faculty leaders whose careers are built through success in academic research and teaching. Further, athletics issues must compete for administrative attention at a given moment with a multitude of competing demands considered more central to the institutional mission. The decisions made under such conditions may set precedents within their own universities or through emulation by others. Under fire, leaders must rely on information immediately available, often carried in the minds of those closest to the decisions, and interpreted through their own life experiences. A web of external commitments, contracts, and customs further circumscribe the options available to decision makers. Only segments of that web are clearly visible to leaders when they must make a decision.

The interaction of the respective processes makes the problems associated with athletics described in prior chapters appear particularly intractable and characterized by systemic inertia. Inertia represents the sum total of myriad forces that hold a system in place and move it, albeit glacially, in a single direction. As documented here and elsewhere, the inertia in college sports has incrementally crept toward both a growing academic-athletic divide and an athletics arms race (toward mythically lucrative programs) that collegiate leaders feel increasingly helpless to address (Atwell, 2001; Campbell, 2000; Duderstadt, 2000). Given the complexities of the issues associated with athletics, no single strategy, individual, or group is likely to be effective in slowing the growth of athletics programs and their aspirations. Instead, effective strategies call for alliances among reform-minded stakeholders across institutional sectors and a variety of approaches to change.

Figure 1 illustrates the interaction of a variety of external forces on decision making related to intercollegiate athletics. Loosely connected boxes represent the structural, legal-regulatory, sociocultural, and economic contexts affecting athletics within which the college or university functions. The diagram shows athletics conferences and the NCAA as relatively autonomous organizations with strong linkages to colleges and universities. The college or university itself is made up of relatively autonomous units of which athletics is one. These units themselves connect to the various external contexts. The figure also shows the impact of the economic context, with resources flowing from media contracts, donors, corporate sponsors, and purveyors of goods and services. The legal and regulatory context acts on colleges and universities with feedback through assorted professional associations and the NCAA. The broader social and cultural context encompasses a variety of dominant and subdominant attitudes and values regarding sports, higher education, gender, race, and sexual orientation. Boundaries among the elements are relatively permeable, if not actively porous, with relatively independent interactions occurring among the various elements. As noted previously, we can view the university as interacting with this complex environment through a variety of channels and representing various offices, responsibilities, and personnel.

FIGURE 1
A Model of Environment-Institutional Interaction

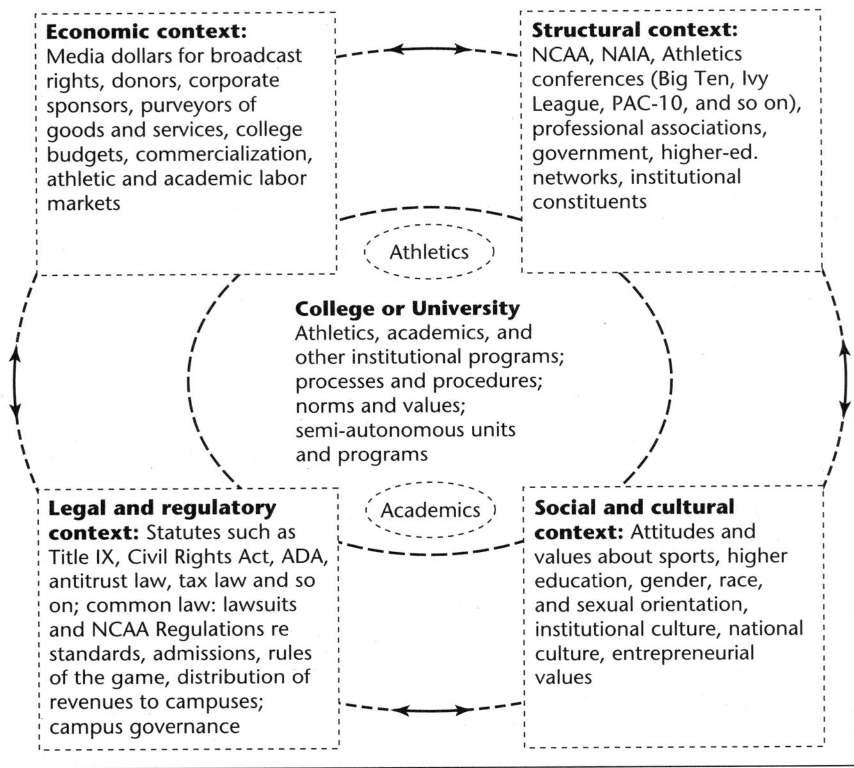

Notes: NCAA = National Collegiate Athletic Association; NAIA = National Association of Intercollegiate Athletics; ADA = Americans with Disabilities Act

This highly simplified representation illustrates the complexity of the organizational environment affecting intercollegiate athletics (or any comparable collaborative endeavor reaching from a college or university). Many elements are beyond the control of the presidents, boards, athletics administrators, and faculty typically challenged to reform athletics. The figure also illustrates the relatively loose coupling among the various forces. For example, media contracts through the NCAA and athletics conferences affect campus programs through their impact on resource flow; rules changes may affect game times, visibility, and promotion of a brand identity in the public arena.

Observations, Themes, and Recommendations

This analysis reveals a set of observations or themes about the power of external influences on college and university decision making and culture related to intercollegiate sports. Although illuminating the significant influence that external factors exert, the observations do not imply that the current role of athletics in higher education is unchangeable. They do demonstrate, however, that faced with loosely coupled processes allowing efforts in one area to be isolated, successful reform requires multipronged strategies ideally based in coalitions to consolidate influence. In other words, no one thing will significantly change this complex system.

Structural Processes

The formal organization of an entity includes reporting structures, mission, decision making, formal lines of communication, staffing, planning, directing, and budgeting. We have seen a number of structural layers related to college sports, including campus, conference, and national associations. Further agreements and formal arrangements structure the collaboration among the many different organizations required for the delivery of intercollegiate athletics. Powerful conference and national associations shape rules and incentives for membership in these organizations that are viewed as central to potentially lucrative postseason play. A number of recommendations are implicit, using levers associated with the structuring of colleges and universities internally and the structures associated with intercollegiate athletics externally. The following recommendations, associated with specific observations and themes, aim to strengthen campus, conference, and association alignment with the academic mission of their host campuses.

- Boards, presidents, and athletics directors can be clear and consistent in their expectations and responses for the quality of the student-athlete experience, ethical conduct, and behavioral standards at every level related to intercollegiate athletics.
- Presidents, athletics directors, and faculty leaders can seek opportunities to integrate athletics staff effectively in the everyday life of the institution. This could involve recognizing the work that coaches do related to other

offices in the university. Thus athletics recruiting could be recognized as an admissions function in which the coach is trained by and represents the admissions office with a charge to broaden recruitment in high school visits to include interested nonathletes. Similarly, fundraising and sports information staff could share training and responsibilities with development and external relations offices. Correspondingly, institutions should seek similar opportunities to engage athletics professionals in the life of the university at large.

- Leaders should attend to the power of routine decisions to affirm institutional identity and the place of sports within it. Leaders can often make high-leverage changes in low-visibility bureaucratic routines. Budgeting and accounting processes and hiring decisions are two examples of such areas. Steps in the hiring process by boards, presidents, and athletics directors are key opportunities to articulate the place of sports and gain commitment to that vision among those who become part of the team to achieve it. Job descriptions, interviews, and the individuals selected to serve on search committees signal consistency or disarray in institutional values related to athletics. The discussions related to the job description, interviews, and the actual hire provide further opportunity to affirm strong educational and ethical values. Travel policies and outside-earnings policies provide other arenas to normalize athletics within broader institutional policies and culture.

- Campus leadership can clearly communicate priorities and respond to behaviors to assess athletics department and university efforts toward gender and racial equity in hiring patterns, team composition, and cultural climate. When women are coaching men's sports in the same numbers as men currently coach women's sports, and when black coaches are proportionate to the number of black athletes, we will know that institutions have finally broken down the cultural barriers to women and people of color in college sports. By the same token, when the institution actively recruits African American students for their academic attributes and assures full representation of women at every level of the faculty and administration, the athletics department will be more clearly part of a larger institutional culture. If the athletics department more effectively incorporates principles of diversity in its practice, it can become a model for the campus at large.

• Leaders should consider carefully to whom the athletics program reports within the organization. This involves both symbolic and substantive competing issues. If the athletics program has a high budget in a large institution, the institutional stake in the program is very high for purposes of reputation, visibility, institutional integrity, and budget. Reporting to the president can symbolize greater institutional integration and control. It can also assure both relationship building and communication between athletics and the range of divisions reporting to the president. At the same time, a reporting line to the president may communicate status and access elevated above programs more central to the institution's academic mission.

Reporting to a vice president can be as problematic as reporting to the president. The student affairs office, for example, views athletics as an extracurricular activity but ignores the big business, fundraising, and public relations aspects. Reporting to a vice president for business and finance diminishes the educational and student development roles of athletics while acknowledging that college sports are big business. Finally, the fit of athletics with the academic affairs office in institutions with highly commercialized programs would be an odd one. In small programs, such as the pre–Title IX women's model, however, in which sports remain tied with physical education, the fit with academic affairs would be unquestionable. The difficulty in placing athletics within the university structure reflects its historic evolution from a student-sponsored extracurricular activity to a highly commercialized activity central to the institution's identity.

• Leaders should recognize the systemic ties related to athletics issues and potential solutions within the university at large. For example, one important way to deemphasize the role of sports as a key avenue for African American men, and some women, to gain a college education is to enhance opportunities through the front door and to recognize students' other talents for admission and scholarship support. Leaders should demand that the entire university as well as the athletics department assure systemic support if they are recruiting students who are different from the student body at large to help assure full inclusion in student life. This is especially relevant for African American student-athletes on predominantly white campuses.

• Leaders should educate boards well. Know the position of individual board members in relation to athletics. Educate the board as a whole and on a recurring basis about intercollegiate athletics nationally and on your campus specifically. Such discussions should build support for policy directions and prior readiness in the case of major athletics success or scandal. Those appointing board members should be particularly attentive to assure their understanding of the institution's academic mission and their independence from the athletics program.

Political Processes

Political processes involve the use of power, jockeying interests among groups with different beliefs and values, using both formal and informal influence, putting pressures on the organization from external forces. From a political perspective, conflict is normal; outcomes result from resolving conflict, compromising, using pressure groups to constrain formal authority, and building coalitions to pool influence on an issue of common, if temporary, concern (Baldridge, Curtis, Ecker, and Riley, 1977; Birnbaum, 1991).

The porous nature of organizational boundaries provides temptation to centralize and thus control decision making. The history of bureaucracies demonstrates the potential for pathology embedded in that strategy. Instead, we suggest seeking ways to strengthen ties between athletics and the college or university at large to build athletics staff identity with the college or university in the face of strong external ties with the athletics professional and governing organizations. Stronger cultural ties across the college or university also expose more personnel to the views and experience of the athletics enterprise, ideally helping to overcome stereotypes of athletics and student-athletes. Leadership at every level of the institution must play a role in connecting athletics to the institution at large: presidents and their staffs, governing boards, faculty governance and faculty opinion leaders, student government, athletics administrators, alumni associations, and leaders of communities encompassing the campus.

- Leaders should work over time, and in multiple arenas, toward an integrated vision of athletics within the institution. Consistent with recommendations in most reports on intercollegiate athletics, leaders should work in coalition with other institutions and associations to deescalate the athletics arms race and reduce commercialism. The conference level is the most immediate and perhaps most powerful avenue for de-escalation. But of course, leaders should not devote so much time and visibility that they reinforce the perceived symbolic supremacy of athletics. A long-term and highly placed staff person or faculty representative may offer both continuity and independence in engaging with athletics decision making related to external organizations.

• Leaders should be relational. Diverse and strong feelings are related to athletics. Attempts to move a sports program in any direction have been a challenge to some of higher education's strongest presidents. Attempting to do so without coming to know the culture and building relationships among the many stakeholders can invite conflict and even failure.

• Leaders should assertively prioritize the inclusion and success of women, African Americans, and other racial and sexual minorities at every level of the athletics and institutional structure. The academic-athletic divide too easily becomes a racial divide on predominantly white campuses and a gender divide on campuses dominated by male values and leadership. Leaders must set standards and model behavior that view student-athletes first as students, despite demanding athletic schedules, cultures, and services. Institutions should create environments in which professional staff and faculty will not assume the needs of student-athletes will be addressed in the athletic department. The gendered nature of sport is an issue for college sports because of the power associated with the intersection of white male dominance in sports, commerce, and social institutions. Male power in sports results in structures, resources, norms, and rules that marginalize or ignore women's participation and perspectives and perpetuate excessive athletics growth. Leaders can consciously name this dynamic and call upon participants at all levels to help create programs across the institution, including athletics, that serve all students with conscious awareness of gender and race in participation as students, student-athletes, and staff.

Entrepreneurial Processes

"It's the economy, stupid!" anchored Bill Clinton's presidential campaign as its central theme in 1992. Consistent with that theme, economic forces are increasingly driving colleges and universities, and the athletics programs within them, to be proactive in diversifying funding sources and be opportunistic about building new ones. Applying for industrial patents for the products of university research, forming research partnerships with industry and government agencies, and naming grants for athletics facilities all characterize a growing entrepreneurial movement in higher education over the past several decades to advance institutional agendas through diversified, external funding (Bok, 2003; Sporn, 1999; Clark, 2004).

This growing entrepreneurialism may support a climate for financial growth in athletics in the name of competition and hopes for windfalls either in gifts or students. At every level of competition, intercollegiate athletics has seen an escalation of commercialism. Clark (2004, p. 2) identifies several key elements associated with successfully entrepreneurial universities that are typically structured to allow substantial autonomy to loosely coupled units: "a diversified funding base; strengthened steering core; an expanded outreach periphery; a stimulated academic heartland; and an integrated entrepreneurial culture." Although college sports do not thrive financially in the vast majority of colleges and universities supporting them, many programs stake their claim for new resources on enhancing college and university coffers beyond athletics through fundraising and enrollments. Let's look at the implications of entrepreneurialism, its assets, and its risks.

- Accept extramural funding judiciously. Clark's elements (2004) of a strengthened steering core and an integrated entrepreneurial culture speak to the importance of a clear institutional identity to provide a context for both independence and relevance to entrepreneurial units including college sports. Clark's elements would suggest thinking carefully about gifts and conditions for accepting them. Accepting NCAA funds for academic support services, for example, is a good thing on the surface, but it may feed the perception that the institution accords privileges to student-athletes without making a comparable commitment to all students' academic success. Similarly, private gifts for facilities or programs, if not carefully fit into an overall plan assuring gender equity, can escalate later athletics spending needs. Additionally, large gifts towards athletics facilities in the absence of a broader giving context can suggest an institutional priority on athletics at the expense of academics.

- Beware of mission drift. Clark (2004, p. 4) notes that transformative change occurs in entrepreneurial colleges and universities in "cumulative, incremental fashion" through "a flow of small alterations, one after another, that lead in time to a qualitative change in organizational character." Although Clark assumes such change is for the good, he describes the very process that produces athletics and other programs that evolve incrementally over time in ways that academic leadership and communities do not always consciously intend. A key role for the strong, collegial central steering core is holding, contextualizing, and articulating the evolving organizational character. Incremental shifts in what the institution does over time to respond to entrepreneurial opportunity will gradually change its mission, if in subtle ways. Attention to the evolving character can allow for course correction if the mission is shifting in undesirable ways.
- Build budgetary accountability and attend to the balance of resource flows and emphasis on athletics relative to programs that serve nonathletes. Does the institution have strong programs in areas such as theater, service learning, orchestra, and residence life? Does it treat their budget needs comparably?
- Recognize issues in athletics as bellwethers for the campus as a whole in relation to the movement toward more entrepreneurial colleges and universities. Industrial cooperation and federal research grants, for example, offer resources for an investment of institutional resources. Entrepreneurial pressures may be inevitable. However, a long history of such pressures on athletics may provide the university with approaches to prevent unintentionally privileging those engaged in such activities to the disadvantage of those that are equally important but less financially fashionable.

Sociocultural Processes

Processes related to the ways in which gender, race, sexual orientation, and athletics itself are enculturated in our society influence decision making in subtle and often invisible ways. Awareness of the social and cultural context as well as of the variety of relatively independent organizational entities involved with both college sports and higher education itself offers some new implications for leadership. Athletics is a crucible in which race, gender, sexual orientation, and social class come together under the dominance of white, heterosexual, masculine norms and values. To the extent that athletics and institutional leadership reflect similar norms and values, the institution will be vulnerable to blindness to both the opportunities and challenges of fully including fresh perspectives and people central to athletics.

The culture of the institution itself and the broader realm of societal values toward sports further circumscribe athletics-related decisions. Given that the particular social and cultural context varies across institutions, an informed strategy for leadership and reform must account for the local culture. However, the crucible of athletics places new twists on these themes, for example, the simultaneous apparent opportunities for and exploitation of African American student athletes. Athletics programs can offer campus leadership an opportunity for moving toward a more socially just climate or become a highly visible representation of societal prejudices. Presidents, commissions, boards, faculty, and national associations can show leadership in addressing gender, race, and homophobia in college sports. Being aware of the white male values dominating college sports allows leaders to pay conscious attention to their implications for staffing, policies, and recruitment. Some specific recommendations follow:

- Build a culture that expects and values diversity at all levels of the institution, reflecting the students it serves. Simultaneously and consciously observe existing patterns. If women and people of color are not represented in coaching and administrative ranks, expect a change and reward it when it happens. We can assume that entrepreneurial spirits will find it in their interest to be more creative and energetic in search processes if ongoing patterns of success or failure in effective hiring and retention practices affect their budgets.
- Assure that student-athletes of color are an integral part of the institution beyond the athletics department. Many institutions actively seek black athletes who dominate the rosters of basketball and football teams. Yet black head coaches, athletics administrators, and institutional leaders are still rare, despite the high numbers of black student-athletes (Engber, 2004). Black student-athletes often find themselves among few black students on predominantly white campuses, except within the athletics department. Given the

historic dynamics of race in the United States and the invisibility and unconscious seductiveness of white privilege, boards, presidents, faculty, and student leaders must be vigilant. Questions they might address include the following: Are minority student-athletes representative of the student body at large? If not, why not? What strategies could assure better representativeness? The goal of such vigilance is institution-wide commitment and inclusion in relation to students of color to avoid real or perceived exploitation and greater alignment between athletics and campus cultures.

- Attend to policies that lend or deny privilege to any group. Allowing car dealers to provide coaches with cars, granting country club memberships, and elaborately appointing offices for sports personnel without giving comparable privileges to other groups puts the athletics personnel on a pedestal. The manner of reducing privileges, however, is as important as the outcome and is a test of executive statesmanship and authority. Experiences on numerous campuses in response to Native American activism and campus awareness and sensitivity in response to the use of Indian mascots have illustrated the importance of being sensitive in diminishing white privilege. Some campuses have handled a change in mascots gracefully with engagement and communication among all concerned groups. Others have resisted change. Still others have attempted change that has failed in the face of opposition from students, board, the public, or faculty.

Symbolic Processes

Symbolic processes involve the ways in which symbols come to be used to ascribe meaning to things or to represent an abstract concept by something concrete. We have seen the use of college sports to concretely represent to the public an institution that otherwise thrives on abstraction. The institution, however, has little control over the meanings that various groups and individuals ascribe to its athletics programs. Depending on social and cultural experience, different groups may ascribe different meanings to the same symbols associated with athletics, or indeed with the symbolism of athletics itself.

Elements of the social and cultural context permeate the system, creating tensions related to gender, race, and sexual orientation at a societal level and related to the institution's academic mission at the campus level. Yet the social and cultural context is least addressed in the literature related to athletics policy, most invisible to participants, and of sufficient weight in the inertia marking the institution of athletics as to affect negatively the likelihood of success for given reform strategies. For example, insufficient awareness, consideration, and consultation related to racial implications of NCAA regulations nearly derailed academic reforms related to admissions standards. Clumsy attempts to either keep or eliminate Native American mascots without understanding and educating the community about the damaging and insulting implications of the mascots offer a second example.

Professional associations, representing additional groupings of external stakeholders, serve to cement relationships and professional identities, develop policy positions relative to a variety of issues at institutional or association levels, and socialize new members of the profession. Professional associations influence campus decision making through the perspectives of members employed on a given campus rather than directly. Athletics professionals reflected in roles from athletics director to coaches, events managers, academic student support services, sports information, and compliance staff deal daily with the campus athletics effort. They develop professionally through that work and through interaction with colleagues doing similar work. Their perspectives and interpretations are likely to be shaped by their athletics experience rather than by broader academic priorities. Yet they are the experts to whom campus leaders turn for information-based decision making. As a result, decisions that may have important cross-institutional effects and symbolism are primarily informed by an increasingly commercialized athletics system rather than one comparably informed by academic and student affairs expertise.

- Use both athletics successes and traumas as opportunities to advance an agenda of increased communication and integration. Both successes and traumas provide opportunities for symbolizing the place and expectations for athletics within the larger institution. Silence especially in the face of trauma can symbolize an absence of institutional control or responsibility for the endeavor, further distancing athletics from the institutional core.
- Use the symbolic power of the office to influence opinion and culture related to athletics as one part of an academic institution. Recognize low-profile

men's and women's sports as well as the command performances at football and basketball games. Take every opportunity to provide incentives and recognition for academic achievement of student-athletes as well as students who are not participants in sports.

• An institutional, faculty, student, or athletics leader should be an anthropologist as well as a manager, economist, and politician. The social and cultural context is the invisible but perhaps most powerful element constraining decision making and leadership related to athletics. Determined boards may encourage decisive action to either control athletics or assure wins regardless of the cost. However, gaining an understanding of the cultural context, which must be at the heart of change, takes time and observation. Many reform efforts are derailed for a failure to understand the cultural context and to build the relationships to influence it. An understanding of the place of men's and women's athletics in the campus culture in all its diversity is a necessary foundation for considering change. A leader's role as anthropologist can be a vehicle for engaging in a low-key, nonadversarial campus discussion regarding the nature and place of athletics on the campus.

The long-term nature of contracts and commitments related to athletics, whether bonds for facilities construction or long-term media contracts, further constrains the decision-making flexibility of those with formal leadership roles, especially when their tenure in office may be less than the duration of those construction or media contracts and commitments.

Systemic Loose Coupling

The strength of a college or university is partially tied to structures that provide the autonomy for creative professionals to pursue questions that extend the boundaries of knowledge. Such systems, however, present challenges for leadership that can rely only lightly on top-down authority. Effective leaders in university settings know well how to use the system to advantage. In relation to athletics, their experience provides a number of strategies.

• Use unanticipated events to nudge the system toward a vision of athletics consistent with a clear institutional identity.

• Be attentive to occasions to assert and reinforce expectations for the quality of the student-athlete experience, ethical conduct, and behavioral standards at every level related to intercollegiate athletics.

• Boards, presidents, vice presidents, athletics directors, and faculty leadership can surround themselves with voices that will provide experiences, perspectives, and knowledge from other leaders. In making decisions under constraints, they will represent the immediate information and memory pool, possibly allowing a broader range of options than like-minded advisers. Diversity, especially of gender and race, may allow decision making that is proactive in a fully inclusive, nonexploitative program despite a societal context that might not be predisposed to full inclusion.

• Be realistic: turning back the clock is not an option. The passion for sports in our society has certainly spilled over to an increasingly commercialized endeavor on our campuses. Although there appears to be a strong consensus that commercialism and the related athletics arms race are out of hand, many interrelated forces have brought the institution of college sports where it is today. To turn back the clock to an ideal that may well never have existed, rather than moving toward a new vision, risks ignoring some of the effects of that evolution, especially in providing educational opportunities for African American, first-generation, and women student-athletes. In many cases, some of these students would have been denied the possibility of a college education in the absence of the scholarships they earn through athletics.

• Collegial values and processes can improve decision making and provide a basis for bridging athletics-academic gulfs.

• Apply learning from athletics to the institution as a whole. Is the athletics department more successful than admissions in recruiting a diverse student population? Are student-athletes graduating in higher proportions than the student body at large? How can those successes inform other programs within the institution?

• Use decision-making issues and processes as opportunities to bring together faculty, administrators, and athletics professionals to hear other perspectives. It becomes difficult to demonize and stereotype when the actors become real people. Furthermore, their involvement can strengthen identification with the institution when professional lives rewarded by entrepreneurial achievement are drawn to identify externally.

- Be humble—neither gloat in success nor despair over failure. The forces supporting the current state of intercollegiate athletics are far more powerful than a single president, athletics director, or even campus. Success, like failure, may be as much a product of its time and the confluence of events as it is a product of individual efforts.

Conclusion

The forces external to the college or university affecting intercollegiate athletics are immense and are not neatly categorized or ordered. Commerce, culture, laws and regulations, collaborative structures, and the politics of their interaction cumulated over time make prospects for rightsizing athletics daunting at best. In the ongoing saga of unsuccessful attempts to reform college sports, we often lose sight of the fact that there have been pockets of progress, if not success. Some colleges and universities, historically among big-time sports institutions, have downsized their sports commitments or restrained their escalation. The Ivies, the military academies, and some of the major research universities such as the University of Chicago were all considered among major football powers at one time and chose to deemphasize (or not escalate) their major sports programs. Although still subject to the cultural effects of athletics recruiting, these institutions have moved from the spotlight related to concerns regarding excesses in athletics to institutions with very distinct identities independent of athletics.

A Harvard or a Chicago has the luxury of a strong public identity supported by a strong resource base. Nevertheless, there is a lesson in terms of the importance of working to build a brand identity of which athletics may be a part but not the dominant vehicle for external recognition. In the face of ambiguity in mission and outcomes associated with higher education, successful major sports teams can rally a university community otherwise fragmented in many ways. Using sports to rally support can produce a tiger whose tail is in the hands of campus leadership, offering support to an athletics juggernaut at the expense of academic programs. The greater leadership challenge is to build a strong campus identity with athletics as an integral rather than dominant part.

This analysis has expanded and integrated semi-independent streams of literatures related to intercollegiate athletics. The exercise does not necessarily raise hope for a deescalation of the forces promoting the overemphasis and commercialization of college sports. Indeed, it may make the challenge seem more difficult. The dynamics producing the escalation are important to understand as colleges and universities become increasingly entrepreneurial in the quest for financial solvency. These dynamics may appear inevitable given changing patterns of funding. However, institutions run a risk by accepting external dollars to support research and service, funding that can become another tiger's tail that influences institutional priorities. The experience of athletics signals the importance of vigilance.

This work does not end with a definitive prognosis for the future of intercollegiate athletics and their impact on colleges and universities. Instead, we pose three scenarios related to the entrepreneurial nature of intercollegiate athletics and the modern university.

The first is unbridled entrepreneurialism, in which each unit rises or sinks on its own, based on its ability to appeal to external funding. A weak institutional core identity or weak central control allows an unfettered exploration and growth depending on market fashions. The contribution to the institution is measured in dollars rather than educational value; and within the institution at large, as well as within the athletics department, external markets and publics define the winners and losers. Within athletics, on a given campus spectator sports are likely to be viewed as the winners, as are the few large institutions where athletics is big and lucrative business within the broader realm of higher education.

The second is rampant bureaucracy, a reliance on rules and oversight evolved to assure a common, focused institutional mission. The rules become so burdensome that they stifle initiative and creativity for adaptation to a changing resource environment. In a sense, the rules become ends in themselves rather than a means toward a more unified culture. The response to creative deviance is to create more rules to fill the loopholes. As the rules become a web too complex to follow, they, too, contribute to organizational pathology focused on compliance and dealing with conscious and inadvertent violations.

The third scenario is an institution in which leadership and participants are proactively responsive and culturally limited in their approach to external opportunity. In other words, a culture represented by strong, clearly held values that the community shares provides symbolic unity even while individual units, including athletics, respond to market opportunities consistent with the values. This approach is the most challenging for leadership because it requires the hard relational work involved with building or reinforcing culture and values across the diverse disciplines and programs that constitute a college or university. More than any other scenario, it calls for a vision of leadership that is dependent not on a single person but on a shared culture that produces appropriate leadership. When boards, faculty, administrators, and students all share a culture, a change in leadership does not represent a breakdown in the glue holding the culture together.

Regardless of the scenario, given the increasingly entrepreneurial nature of colleges and universities, athletics has been a precursor to a broader institutional entrepreneurialism. Athletics represents the arena in which U.S. colleges and universities have long worked to balance institutional goals and values with external markets. Athletics may demonstrate the power of the external environment, but it also demonstrates the stake and importance of integrating with a strong, core institutional culture, assuring athletics' fit with and contribution to a healthy and enduring institutional identity.

References

Acosta, R. V., and Carpenter, L. J. (1985). Women in sport. In D. Chu, J. O. Segrave, and B. J. Becker (Eds.), *Sport and higher education.* Champaign, IL: Human Kinetics.

Acosta, R. V., and Carpenter, L. J. (2004). *Women in intercollegiate sport: A longitudinal study—twenty-seven-year update 1977–2004.* http://webpages.charter.net/womeninsport. Retrieved June 9, 2004.

American Institutes for Research (AIR). (1989). *The experiences of black intercollegiate athletes at NCAA Division I institutions* (Report No. 3). Palo Alto, CA: Center for the Study of Athletics.

Americans with Disabilities Act of 1990. 42 U.S.C. §12101 et seq.

Anderson, D. F., and Gill, K. S. (1983). Occupational socialization patterns of men's and women's interscholastic basketball coaches. *Journal of Sport Behaviors, 6*(3), 105–116.

Association of Governing Boards (AGB). (2004). *Statement on board responsibilities for intercollegiate athletics.* Washington, DC: Association of Governing Boards of Colleges and Universities.

Association for Intercollegiate Athletics for Women (AIAW) v. NCAA, 559 F. Supp. 487 (D.C.C. 1983), 735 F. 2n 577 (D.C. Cir. 1984).

Atwell, R. H. (2001). The only way to reform college sports is to embrace commercialization. *Chronicle of Higher Education, 47*(44), B20.

Bachin, R. F. (2001). Courage, endurance and quickness of decision: Gender and athletics at the University of Chicago, 1890–1920. *Rethinking History, 5*(1), 93–116.

Bailey, W. S., and Littleton, T. D. (1991). *Athletics and academe: An anatomy of abuses and a prescription for reform.* New York: Macmillan. (ED 328 156, HE 024 209)

Baldridge, J. V., Curtis, D. V., Ecker, G. P., and Riley, G. L. (1977). Alternative models of governance in higher education. In G. L. Riley and J. V. Baldridge (Eds.), *Governing academic organizations.* Berkeley, CA: McCutchan.

Birnbaum, R. (1991). *How colleges work: The cybernetics of academic organization and leadership.* San Francisco: Jossey-Bass.

Blum, D. E. (1994). College sports' L-word. *Chronicle of Higher Education, 40*(27), A35–36. (EJ 479 665)

Blum, D. E. (1995a). Beyond the big time. *Chronicle of Higher Education, 41*(23), A39.

Blum, D. E. (1995b). Brown loses bias case. *Chronicle of Higher Education, 41*(30), A37–38. (EJ 501 649)

Bok, D. (2003). *Universities in the marketplace: The commercialization of higher education.* Princeton, NJ: Princeton University Press.

Bonnette, V. M., and Daniel, L. (1990). *Title IX athletics investigator's manual.* Washington, DC: U.S. Department of Education, Office of Civil Rights. (ED 400 763)

Bowen, W. G., and Levin, S. A. (2003). *Reclaiming the game: College sports and educational values.* Princeton, NJ: Princeton University Press.

Byers, W., with Hammer, C. (1995). *Unsportsmanlike conduct: Exploiting college athletes.* Ann Arbor: University of Michigan Press.

Cahn, S. K. (1994). *Coming on strong: Gender and sexuality in twentieth-century women's sport.* Cambridge, MA: Harvard University Press.

Campbell, J. R. (2000). *Dry rot in the ivory tower: A case for fumigations, ventilation, and renewal of the academic sanctuary.* New York: University Press of America.

Chu, D. (1989). *The character of American higher education and intercollegiate sport.* Albany: State University of New York Press.

Civil Rights Act of 1964, PL 88-352, 78 Stat. 241 (1964).

Civil Rights Restoration Act of 1987, PL 100-259, 102 Stat. 18 (1988).

Clark, B. R. (1998). *Creating entrepreneurial universities: Organizational pathways of transformation.* Oxford: IAU Press/Pergamon.

Clark, B. R. (2004). *Sustaining change in universities: Continuities in case studies and concepts.* Berkshire, UK: Open University Press.

Coalition on Intercollegiate Athletics (COIA). (Sept. 15, 2004). *About the coalition.* http://www.math.umd.edu/~jmc/COIA/COIA-Home.html. Retrieved Dec. 9, 2004.

Cohen v. Brown University, 879 F.Supp. 185, 214 D.R.I. (1995).

Cohen, M. D., and March, J. G. (1974). *Leadership and ambiguity: The American college president.* New York: McGraw-Hill.

Connell, R. W. (1995). *Masculinities.* Berkeley: University of California Press.

Creedon, P. J. (1994). Women, media and sport: Creating and reflecting gender values. In P. J. Creedon (Ed.), *Women, media and sport: Challenging gender values.* Thousand Oaks, CA: Sage.

Creedon, P. J., Cramer, J. A., and Granitz, E. H. (1994). Pandering or empowering? Economics and promotion of women's sport. In P. J. Creedon (Ed.), *Women, media and sport: Challenging gender values.* Thousand Oaks, CA: Sage.

de Varona, D., and Foudy, J. (2003). *Minority views on the report of the Commission on Opportunity in Athletics.* Washington, DC: U.S. Department of Education.

Department of Health, Education, and Welfare, Office of Civil Rights. (1979). Title IX of the Education Amendments of 1972; A policy interpretation; Title IX and intercollegiate athletics. *Federal Register, 44*(239). Dec. 11, 1979.

DiBiaggio, J. (1991). Cosmetic change vs. real reform. *Academe, 77*(1), 21–22.

Drake Group. (2004). The Drake Group mission. http://www.thedrakegroup.org. Retrieved Dec. 12, 2004.

Duderstadt, J. D. (2000). *Intercollegiate athletics and the American university: A university president's perspective.* Ann Arbor: University of Michigan Press.

Edwards, H. (1984). The black "dumb jock": An American sports tragedy. *College Board Review,* no. 131, 8–13.

Engber, D. (2004). Lack of diversity among Division I is reflected in football coaches they hire, says scholar. *Chronicle of Higher Education, 51*(14), A34.

Festle, M. J. (1996). *Playing nice: Politics and apologies in women's sports.* New York: Columbia University Press.

Fleisher, A. A., III, Goff, B. L., and Tollison, R. D. (1992). *The National Collegiate Athletic Association: A study in cartel behavior.* Chicago: University of Chicago Press.

Franklin v. Gwinnett County Public Schools. (1992). 112 S.Ct. 1028.

Frey, J. H. (1985). College athletics: Problems of institutional control. In D. Chu, J. O. Segrave, and B. J. Becker (Eds.), *Sport and higher education.* Champaign, IL: Human Kinetics.

Frey, J. H. (Ed.). (1982). *The governance of intercollegiate athletics.* West Point, NY: Leisure Press.

Fulks, D. L. (2002a). *Revenues and expenses of Divisions I and II intercollegiate athletics programs: Financial trends and relationships—2001.* Indianapolis: National Collegiate Athletic Association.

Fulks, D. L. (2002b). *Revenues and expenses of Division III intercollegiate athletics programs: Financial trends and relationships—2001.* Indianapolis: National Collegiate Athletic Association.

Gerber, E. W. (1975). The controlled development of collegiate sport for women: 1923–1936. *Journal of Sports History, 2*(2), 1–28.

Gerdy, J. R. (2001). Facing up to the conflict between athletics and academics. *AGB Priorities, 16,* 12. (ED 453 750)

Gerdy, J. R. (2002). *Sports: An all-American addiction.* Jackson, MS: University Press of Mississippi.

Gouldner, H. (1980). The social impact of campus litigation. *Journal of Higher Education, 51,* 328.

Government Accounting Office (GAO). (2001). *Four-year colleges' experiences adding and discontinuing teams.* Washington, DC: GAO.

Gray, H. (1996). The leaning tower of academe. *Bulletin of the American Academy of Arts and Sciences, 49,* 34–54.

Griffin, P. (1998). *Strong women, deep closets: Lesbians and homophobia in sport.* Champaign, IL: Human Kinetics.

Grove City College v. Bell, 465 U.S. 555 (1984).

Guttman, A. (1982). The tiger devours the literary magazine, or, intercollegiate athletics in America. In J. H. Frey (Ed.), *The governance of intercollegiate athletics.* West Point, NY: Leisure Press.

Guttman, A. (1988). *A whole new ballgame: An interpretation of American sports.* Chapel Hill, NC: University of North Carolina Press.

Guttman, A. (1991). *Women's sports: A history.* New York: Columbia University Press.

Hanford, G. H. (1974). *An inquiry into the need for and feasibility of a national study of intercollegiate athletics.* Washington, DC: American Council on Education.

Hardy, S. H., and Berryman, J. W. (1982). A historical view of the governance issue. In J. H. Frey (Ed.), *The governance of intercollegiate athletics.* West Point, NY: Leisure Press.

Henry, D. D. (1975). *Challenges past, challenges present: An analysis of American higher education since 1930.* San Francisco: Jossey-Bass.

Hesburgh, T., and Alvino, J. (1995). Reform and renewal in college sports. *Journal of College and University Law, 22*(1), 63–76. (EJ 516 488)

Hobbs, W. C. (1981). The courts. In P. G. Altbach and R. O. Berdahl (Eds.), *Higher education in American society.* Amherst, NY: Prometheus Books.

Hult, J. S. (1999). NAGWS and AIAW: The strange and wondrous journey to the athletic summit, 1950–1990. *Journal of Physical Education, Recreation and Dance, 70*(4), 24–32.

Jacobson, J. (2001). Colleges cut men's teams. *Chronicle of Higher Education, 47*(28), A44.

Jacobson, J. (2002). Rice U. football coach chastised for comments on gay athletes. *Chronicle of Higher Education, 49*(11), A38.

Johnson, A. G. (2001). *Privilege, power, and difference.* New York: McGraw-Hill Higher Education.

Kane, M. J. (2001). Leadership, sport, and gender. In S.J.M. Freeman, S. C. Bourque, and C. M. Shelton (Eds.), *Women on power: Leadership redefined.* Boston: Northeastern University Press.

Kaplin, W., and Lee, B. (1995). *The law of higher education.* (3rd ed.) San Francisco: Jossey-Bass.

Kezar, A. (2004). Obtaining integrity? Reviewing and examining the charter between higher education and society. *Review of Higher Education, 27*(4), 429–459.

Kidd, B. (1990). The men's cultural centre: Sports and the dynamic of women's oppression/men's repression. In M. A. Messner and D. F. Sabo (Eds.), *Sport, men and the gender order: Critical feminist perspectives.* Champaign, IL: Human Kinetics.

Knight Foundation Commission on Intercollegiate Athletics (Knight Commission). (1991). *Keeping faith with the student-athlete: A new model for intercollegiate athletics.* Charlotte, NC: John S. and James L. Knight Foundation.

Knight Foundation Commission on Intercollegiate Athletics (Knight Commission). (2001). *A call to action: Reconnecting college sports and higher education.* Charlotte, NC: John S. and James L. Knight Foundation.

Koch, J. V. (1971). The economics of "big-time" intercollegiate athletics. *Social Science Quarterly, 52*(3), 148–260.

Lapchick, R. E. (1996). Race and college sports: A long way to go. In R. E. Lapchick, *Sport in society: Equal opportunity or business as usual?* Thousand Oaks, CA: Sage.

Lapchick, R. E., and Slaughter, J. B. (Eds.). (1994). *The rules of the game: Ethics in college sport.* Phoenix: Oryx Press.

Law v. NCAA. (1998). F.3d., 10th Circuit U.S. App. 134: 1010.

Lederman, D. (1991). Penn State coach's comments about lesbian athletes may be used to test university's new policy on bias. *Chronicle of Higher Education, 37*(38), A27.

Lombardi, J. V., and others. (2003). *The sports imperative in America's research universities. The top American research universities: An annual report.* Gainesville, FL: Lombardi Program on Measuring University Performance.

Lucas, J. A., and Smith, R. A. (1978). *Saga of American sport.* Philadelphia: Lea and Febiger.

McIntosh, P. (1990). White privilege: Unpacking the invisible knapsack. *Independent School, 49*(2), 31–35.

Messner, M. A. (1990). Masculinities and athletic careers: Bonding and status differences. In M. A. Messner and D. F. Sabo (Eds.), *Sport, men, and the gender order: Critical feminist perspectives.* Champaign, IL: Human Kinetics.

Messner, M. A. (2002). *Taking the field: Women, men, and sports.* Sport and Culture Series, Vol. 4. Minneapolis: University of Minnesota Press.

Messner, M. A., and Sabo, D. F. (1994). *Sex, violence, and power in sports: Rethinking masculinity.* Freedom, CA: Crossing Press.

Messner, M. A., and Sabo, D. F. (Eds.). (1990). *Sport, men and the gender order: Critical feminist perspectives.* Champaign, IL: Human Kinetics.

National Association of Intercollegiate Athletics (NAIA). (n.d.). *NAIA coming home: The new NAIA, a proud past, a dynamic future.* http://www.naia.org/campaign/history/history.html. Retrieved Aug. 18, 2002.

National Association of Intercollegiate Athletics (NAIA). (2004). *Sports information directors manual.* Olathe, KS: NAIA.

National Collegiate Athletic Association (NCAA). (2003a). *Factsheet.* Indianapolis: NCAA. http://www1.ncaa.org/membership/ed_outreach/research/Fact_sheets/Fact_Sheet_10–10–03.htm. Retrieved June 12, 2004.

National Collegiate Athletic Association (NCAA). (2003b). *2001–02 Race demographics of NCAA member institutions' athletics personnel: The NCAA Minority Opportunities and Interests Committee's two-year study.* Indianapolis: NCAA.

National Collegiate Athletic Association (NCAA). (2004a). *2004–2005 NCAA Division I manual.* Indianapolis: NCAA.

National Collegiate Athletic Association (NCAA). (2004b). *2004–2005 NCAA Division II manual.* Indianapolis: NCAA.

National Collegiate Athletic Association (NCAA). (2004c). *2004–2005 NCAA Division III manual.* Indianapolis: NCAA.

National Collegiate Athletic Association (NCAA). (2004d). *1999–2000–2002–2003 NCAA Student-Athlete Ethnicity Report.* Indianapolis: NCAA.

National Collegiate Athletic Association (NCAA) Research. (2002). *1982–2001 NCAA sports sponsorship and participation report.* Indianapolis: NCAA.

National Junior College Athletic Association (NJCAA). (n.d.a). About NCJCAA: Purpose papers. http://www.njcaa.org/purpose.cfm. Retrieved Jan. 17, 2005.

National Junior College Athletic Association (NJCAA). (n.d.b). Membership directory. http://www.njcaa.org/membershipdirectory.cfm. Retrieved Jan. 17, 2005.

National Junior College Athletic Association (NJCAA). (n.d.c). *History of the NJCAA.* http://www.njcaa.org/history.cfm. Retrieved July 5, 2002.

National Wrestling Coaches Association v. the US Department of Education. (2004). 366 F.3d 930, 936-40 (DC Cir.).

Naughton, J., and Fiore, M. (1997). Advocacy group charges 25 colleges with violating Title IX in athletics. *Chronicle of Higher Education, 43*(38), A44.

NCAA v. Board of Regents of the University of Oklahoma, 468 U.S. 85 (1984).

NCAA v. Smith. S.Ct, U.S. 525: 459 (1999).

Oglesby, C. A. (2001). Intersections: Women's sport leadership and feminist praxis. In S.J.M. Freeman, S. C. Bourque, and C. M. Shelton (Eds.), *Women on power: Leadership redefined.* Boston: Northeastern University Press.

Pharr, S. (1988). *Homophobia: A weapon of sexism.* Inverness, CA: Chardon Press.

Powell, W. W., and DiMaggio, P. J. (Eds.). (1991). *The new institutionalism in organizational analysis.* Chicago: University of Chicago Press.

Putney, C. (2001). *Muscular Christianity: Manhood and sports in Protestant America, 1880–1920.* Cambridge, MA: Harvard University Press.

Rhodes, T. A., and Gerking, S. (2000). Educational contributions, academic quality, and athletic success. *Contemporary Economic Policy, 18*(20), 248–258.

Rudolph, F. (1990, 1962). *The American college and university: A history.* Athens: University of Georgia Press. (Originally published 1962.)

Sack, A. L. (1982). Cui bono? Contradictions in college sports and athletes' rights. In J. H. Frey (Ed.), *The governance of intercollegiate athletics.* West Point, NY: Leisure Press.

Sack, A. L., and Staurowsky, E. J. (1998). *College athletes for hire: The evolution and legacy of the NCAA's amateur myth.* Westport, CT: Praeger.

Sage, A. L. (1982). The intercollegiate sport cartel and its consequences for athletes. In J. H. Frey (Ed.), *The governance of intercollegiate athletics.* West Point, NY: Leisure Press.

Sage, G. H. (1990). *Power and ideology in American sport: A critical perspective.* Champaign, IL: Human Kinetics.

Savage, H. J., with Bentley, H. W., McGovern J. T., and Smiley, D. G. (1929). *American college athletics* (Bulletin Number Twenty-three). New York: Carnegie Foundation for the Advancement of Teaching.

Scott, W. R. (2001). *Institutions and organizations.* (2nd ed.) Thousand Oaks, CA: Sage.

Sherman Anti-Trust Act. 15 U.S.C. §1. (1973).

Shropshire, K. L. (1996). *In black and white: Race and sports in America.* New York: New York University Press.

Shulman, J. L., and Bowen, W. G. (2001). *The game of life: College sports and educational values.* Princeton: Princeton University Press.

Slatton, B. (1982). AIAW: The greening of American athletics. In J. H. Frey (Ed.), *The governance of intercollegiate athletics.* West Point, NY: Leisure Press.

Smith, R. (1988). *Sports and freedom: The rise of big-time college athletics.* New York: Oxford University Press.

Smith, R. K. (2000). A brief history of the NCAA's role in regulating athletics. *Marquette Law Journal, 11*(1), 9.

Sojka, G. S. (1985). The evolution of the student-athlete in America: From the divinity to the divine. In D. Chu, J. O. Segrave, and B. J. Becker (Eds.), *Sport and higher education.* Champaign, IL: Human Kinetics.

Solomon, B. M. (1985). *In the company of educated women: A history of women and higher education in America.* New Haven, CT: Yale University Press.

Sperber, M. (1990). *College Sports, Inc.: The athletic department vs. the university.* New York: Henry Holt.

Sperber, M. (2000). *Beer and circus: How big-time college sports is crippling undergraduate education.* New York: Henry Holt.

Sporn, B. (1999). *Adaptive university structures: An analysis of adaptation to socioeconomic environments of U.S. and European universities.* London: Jessica Kingsley.

Staurowsky, E. J. (1990). Women coaching male athletes. In Messner, M., and Sabo, D. (Eds.), *Sport, men, and the gender order: Critical feminist perspectives.* Champaign, IL: Human Kinetics.

Staurowsky, E. J. (2002). The relationship between athletics and higher education fund raising: The myths far outweigh the facts. In National Coalition for Women and Girls in Education (NCWGE), *Title IX athletics policies: Issues and data for education decision makers.* Washington, DC: NCWGE. http//www.ncwge.org/Title_IX_Coalition_Report_Final.pdf. Retrieved Sept. 16, 2003.

Steele, C. M. (1997). A threat in the air: How stereotypes shape intellectual identity and performance. *American Psychologist, 52*(6), 613–629.

Stern, R. N. (1979). The development of an interorganizational control network: The case of intercollegiate athletics. *Administrative Science Quarterly, 24,* 242–266.

Stinchcombe, A. L. (1965). Social structure and organization. In J. G. March (Ed.), *Handbook of organizations.* Chicago: Rand McNally.

Suggs, W. (2003a). Conference soap opera is driven by cash, but cachet matters, too. *Chronicle of Higher Education, 49*(38), A37.

Suggs, W. (2003b). In football, the have-nots clash with the haves: Some colleges say they are unfairly shut out of bowl games. *Chronicle of Higher Education, 50*(2), A48.

Suggs, W. (2004a). Mellon fund tackles college sports: New project focuses on academic requirements for athletes and the role of coaches. *Chronicle of Higher Education, 51*(2), A43.

Suggs, W. (2004b). Outside the NCAA: Few sports, fewer women. *Chronicle of Higher Education, 50*(41), A36.

Thelin, J. R. (1994). *Games colleges play: Scandal and reform in intercollegiate athletics.* Baltimore: Johns Hopkins University Press. (ED 403 850)

Thelin, J. R. (1990). Fiscal fitness? The peculiar economics of intercollegiate athletics. *Capital Ideas, 4*(4), 1–12. (ED 323 823)

Thelin, J. R. (2000). Good sports? Historical perspective on the political economy of intercollegiate athletics in the era of Title IX, 1972–1997. *Journal of Higher Education, 71*(4), 391–410.

Thelin, J. R., and Wiseman, L. L. (1989). *The old college try: Balancing academics and athletics in higher education.* ASHE-ERIC Higher Education Report No. 4. Washington, DC: School of Education and Human Development, George Washington University.

Title VI of the Civil Rights Act of 1964, 42 U.S.C. §2000d *et seq.* (1964).

Title IX of the Education Amendments, 20 U.S.C. §1681 *et seq.* (1972).

Toma, J. D. (1999). The collegiate ideal and the tools of external relations: The uses of high-profile intercollegiate athletics. In J. D. Toma and A. J. Kezar (Eds.), *Reconceptualizing the collegiate ideal.* New Directions for Higher Education, no. 105. San Francisco: Jossey-Bass.

Toma, J. D. (2003). *Football U.: Spectator sports in the life of the American university.* Ann Arbor: University of Michigan Press.

Toma, J. D., and Cross, M. E. (1998). Intercollegiate athletics and student college choice: Exploring the impact of championship seasons on undergraduate application. *Research in Higher Education, 39*(2), 633–661.

Tow, T. C. (1982). The governance role of the NCAA. In J. H. Frey (Ed.), *The governance of intercollegiate athletics.* West Point, NY: Leisure Press.

University of Maine. (2004). *2004–05 Men's Ice Hockey Media Guide.* Orono: University of Maine Athletic Media Relations Office.

Veysey, L. R. (1965). *The emergence of the modern university.* Chicago: University of Chicago Press.

Whitson, D. (1990). Sport in the social construction of masculinity. In M. A. Messner and D. F. Sabo (Eds.), *Sport, men, and the gender order: Critical feminist perspectives.* Champaign, IL: Human Kinetics.

Wiggins, D. K. (1991). Prized performers, but frequently overlooked students: The involvement of black athletes in intercollegiate sports on predominantly white university campuses, 1890–1972. *Research Quarterly for Exercise and Sport, 62*(2), 164–177. (EJ 433 750)

Wolf-Wendel, L. E., Toma, D. J., and Morphew, C. C. (2001). How much difference is too much difference? Perceptions of gay men and lesbians in intercollegiate athletics. *Journal of College Student Development, 42*(5), 465–479.

Wong, G. (1994). *Essentials of amateur sports law.* (2nd ed.) Westport, CT: Praeger.

Wu, Y. (1999). Early NCAA attempts at governance of women's intercollegiate athletics, 1968–1973. *Journal of Sport History, 26*(3), 585.

Wushanley, Y. (2004). *Playing nice and losing: The struggle for control of women's athletics, 1960–2000.* Syracuse, N.Y.: Syracuse University Press.

Zimbalist, A. (1999). *Unpaid professionals: Commercialism and conflict in big-time college sports.* Princeton, NJ: Princeton University Press.

Zipter, Y. (1988). *Diamonds are a dyke's best friend: Reflections, reminiscences, and reports from the field on the lesbian national pastime.* Ithaca, NY: Firebrand Books.

Name Index

V

W

Z

Subject Index

S

T

V

W

About the Authors

Suzanne E. Estler is associate professor of higher educational leadership at the University of Maine, where she served for over a decade as director of equal opportunity and Title IX coordinator. She holds a Ph.D. in educational administration and policy analysis from Stanford University and an M.A. in human relations/student affairs from Ohio University. She also holds a B.A. from Douglass College. Her scholarship focuses on the intersection among diversity, privilege, and colleges and universities as complex organizations; her current interests are intercollegiate athletics, culture, and leadership.

Laurie J. Nelson is a graduate student in student development in higher education at the University of Maine. She holds a B.A. from Bowdoin College and an M.A. in sociology from the University of Notre Dame, where her thesis explored masculinity and skateboarding culture. Intercollegiate athletics is one aspect of her scholarly interests in gender, identity, and social institutions.

About the ASHE Higher Education Reports Series

Since 1983, the ASHE (formerly ASHE-ERIC) Higher Education Report Series has been providing researchers, scholars, and practitioners with timely and substantive information on the critical issues facing higher education. Each monograph presents a definitive analysis of a higher education problem or issue, based on a thorough synthesis of significant literature and institutional experiences. Topics range from planning to diversity and multiculturalism, to performance indicators, to curricular innovations. The mission of the Series is to link the best of higher education research and practice to inform decision making and policy. The reports connect conventional wisdom with research and are designed to help busy individuals keep up with the higher education literature. Authors are scholars and practitioners in the academic community. Each report includes an executive summary, review of the pertinent literature, descriptions of effective educational practices, and a summary of key issues to keep in mind to improve educational policies and practice.

The Series is one of the most peer reviewed in higher education. A National Advisory Board made up of ASHE members reviews proposals. A National Review Board of ASHE scholars and practitioners reviews completed manuscripts. Six monographs are published each year and they are approximately 120 pages in length. The reports are widely disseminated through Jossey-Bass and John Wiley & Sons, and they are available online to subscribing institutions through Wiley InterScience (http://www.interscience.wiley.com).

Call for Proposals

The ASHE Higher Education Report Series is actively looking for proposals. We encourage you to contact one of the editors, Dr. Kelly Ward (kaward@wsu.edu) or Dr. Lisa Wolf-Wendel (lwolf@ku.edu), with your ideas.

Recent Titles

Volume 30 ASHE-ERIC Higher Education Reports

1. Governance in the Twenty-First Century: Approaches to Effective Leadership and Strategic Management
   Dennis John Gayle, Bhoendradatt Tewarie, and A. Quinton White, Jr.
2. Retaining Minority Students in Higher Education
   Watson Scott Swail with Kenneth E. Redd and Laura W. Perna
3. Understanding and Reducing College Student Departure
   John M. Braxton, Amy S. Hirschy, and Shederick A. McClendon
4. Accreditation Matters: Achieving Academic Recognition and Renewal
   Jeffrey W. Alstete

Volume 29 ASHE-ERIC Higher Education Reports

1. Ensuring Quality and Productivity in Higher Education: An Analysis of Assessment Practices
   Susan M. Gates and Associates
2. Institutionalizing a Broader View of Scholarship Through Boyer's Four Domains
   John M. Braxton, William Luckey, and Patricia Helland
3. Transforming the Curriculum: Preparing Students for a Changing World
   Elizabeth A. Jones
4. Quality in Distance Education: Focus on On-Line Learning
   Katrina A. Meyer
5. Faculty Service Roles and the Scholarship of Engagement
   Kelly Ward
6. Identity Development of Diverse Populations: Implications for Teaching and Administration in Higher Education
   Vasti Torres, Mary F. Howard-Hamilton, Diane L. Cooper

Volume 28 ASHE-ERIC Higher Education Reports

1. The Changing Nature of the Academic Deanship
   Mimi Wolverton, Walter H. Gmelch, Joni Montez, and Charles T. Nies
2. Faculty Compensation Systems: Impact on the Quality of Higher Education
   Terry P. Sutton, Peter J. Bergerson
3. Socialization of Graduate and Professional Students in Higher Education: A Perilous Passage?
   John C. Weidman, Darla J. Twale, Elizabeth Leahy Stein
4. Understanding and Facilitating Organizational Change in the 21st Century: Recent Research and Conceptualizations
   Adrianna J. Kezar
5. Cost Containment in Higher Education: Issues and Recommendations
   Walter A. Brown, Cayo Gamber
6. Facilitating Students' Collaborative Writing
   Bruce W. Speck

Back Issue/Subscription Order Form

Copy or detach and send to:
Jossey-Bass, A Wiley Imprint, 989 Market Street, San Francisco CA 94103-1741

Call or fax toll-free: Phone 888-378-2537 6:30AM – 3PM PST; Fax 888-481-2665

Back Issues: Please send me the following issues at $24 each
(Important: please include series abbreviation and issue number. For example AEHE 28:1)

____

____

____

$ __________ Total for single issues

$ __________ SHIPPING CHARGES:

SURFACE	Domestic	Canadian
First Item	$5.00	$6.00
Each Add'l Item	$3.00	$1.50

For next-day and second-day delivery rates, call the number listed above

Subscriptions Please ❑ start ❑ renew my subscription to *ASHE-ERIC Higher Education Reports* for the year 2_____at the following rate:

U.S.	❑ Individual $165	❑ Institutional $175
Canada	❑ Individual $165	❑ Institutional $235
All Others	❑ Individual $213	❑ Institutional $286

❑ Online subscriptions available too!

For more information about online subscriptions visit www.interscience.wiley.com

$ __________ Total single issues and subscriptions (Add appropriate sales tax for your state for single issue orders. No sales tax for U.S. subscriptions. Canadian residents, add GST for subscriptions and single issues.)

❑Payment enclosed (U.S. check or money order only)
❑VISA ❑ MC ❑ AmEx ❑ #____________________ Exp. Date ______

Signature ________________________ Day Phone __________
❑ Bill Me (U.S. institutional orders only. Purchase order required.)

Purchase order # ______________________________
Federal Tax ID13559302 **GST 89102 8052**

Name ______________________________________

Address _____________________________________

____

Phone ____________________ E-mail ________________________

For more information about Jossey-Bass, visit our Web site at www.josseybass.com